D0999750

BANNOCKBURN

The Battle for a Nation

BANNOCKBURN

The Battle for a Nation

ALISTAIR MOFFAT

BIRLINN

First published in 2014 by
Birlinn Limited
West Newington House
10 Newington Road
Edinburgh
EH9 1QS

www.birlinn.co.uk

ISBN: 978 1 78027 218 4

British Library Cataloguing-in-Publication Data
A catalogue record for this book is available
from the British Library

Designed by James Hutcheson
Typeset by Mark Blackadder

Endpapers: The Battle of Bannockburn from The Holkham Bible
(© The British Library Board, ADD47682)

Printed and bound by Grafica Veneta
www.graificaveneta.com

For my son,
ADAM MOFFAT

and his fiancée,
KIM McCALLUM

2014 is also their year

Bannockburn

How can I sing of so much blood?

Great battles loom over our childhoods. We name them
With mountains and seas. We copy out their cause.

But a banner is not a battle. This soft landscape too
Has become forgetful – wildflower, woodlight, fresh snow.

Yet once, beneath peat and clay here, the vaulted hull
Of a whale sang in waves to its mate. And once flesh

Gave beneath foot here, over park, carse and burn.
Below a clear summer sky, blood-flecked linnets

Flit between the mouths of the dead and dying,
While they sing of the mercilessness – the pity of it all.

TOM POW

(Epigraph from *The Battle of Bannockburn* by Robert Baston, translated from the Latin by Edwin Morgan. Commissioned by the National Trust for Scotland as one of ten poems to mark the renovation of the Rotunda at the Bannockburn site in 2014)

Contents

Preface

2014 sees the 700th anniversary of the Battle of Bannockburn, one of the few events that genuinely changed the direction of Scotland's history. Its outcome was far from inevitable, indeed it was a remarkably unlikely victory. Defeat for King Robert and his famous captains might have seen a union of the crowns three centuries before James VI became James I. And instead of a Scots king riding south to rule in England, an English king may have come north to be crowned at Scone, or may have simply adopted the title without any ceremony. The consequences of that dynastic traffic could have been far-reaching in the shaping of modern Scotland. Wales had been brutally absorbed by Edward I and his successors as it became England's first colony. If the English cavalry and their deadly archers had broken the ranks of the Scottish schiltrons in 1314, Scotland may well have become a second colony, and as happened in Wales, few of its distinctive institutions would have survived.

2014 is more than the anniversary of a battle, it is also the year of Scotland. With the Commonwealth Games in Glasgow and the Ryder Cup at Gleneagles, images of Scotland and the joy and drama of sport will be broadcast all around the world. In September 2014, the eyes of the world will again be on this small nation as its people decide on its future. The question posed in the referendum offers a stark choice: do Scots wish to remain in the union with England, Wales and Northern Ireland, or do they wish to live in an independent country? Seven centuries ago a very different sort of campaign on the issue of Scotland's independence came to its climax at Bannockburn when, as one chronicler put it, 'After the aforesaid victory Robert de Brus was commonly called King of Scotland by all men, because he had acquired Scotland by force of arms.' For many reasons 2014 seems an appropriate moment to remember how he did it.

That was certainly the view of Hugh Andrew of Birlinn. This book is his direct commission, and what an excellent choice of subject. Like most Scots, I knew a little about Bannockburn but until I began to read in some depth, I had no idea what a remarkable, genuinely stirring story it is. Throughout my research I continually referred to the work of a very great scholar. G.W.S. Barrow's *Robert Bruce and the Community of the Realm of Scotland* is a masterpiece as it deals with Bruce's reign and his extraordinary rise from a guerrilla fighter in the Galloway Hills to become the victor of Bannockburn. This book deals only with the battle, but if what follows stimulates a thirst for more, then G.W.S. Barrow's great work is unsurpassed.

In addition to Hugh Andrew, I want to thank the team at Birlinn: Jan Rutherford, Andrew Simmons, Jim Hutcheson, Liz Short and Anna Renz are all a joy to work with and all absolute professionals. And my agent, lovely David Godwin, came up to Edinburgh to pilot this and other projects through a very cheery and creative dinner. Sitting at a desk in the pool of anglepoise light on a dark, stormy morning at the end of December 2013, working alone in my office, it is more than a comfort to know that David and all at Birlinn are working alongside me to convert myriad sheaves of scribbled and badly typed pages into very good-looking books. Thank you to all for your many kindnesses and great forbearance.

Finally I want to record my thanks to one of Scotland's greatest contemporary poets for allowing me to begin this book with his superb poem about Bannockburn. It sparkles with sharp observation, is concise and simply written. It warms my heart to see our work in the same book and the poem catches much of the spirit of what I hoped to convey.

Alistair Moffat
SELKIRK
27 December 2013

I

The Night Before the Morning

Vigils, the Feast of St John the Baptist, in the Year of Our Lord, 1314, the Sixth Year of the reign of Edward, Second of that name, King of England, Lord of Ireland, Duke of Aquitaine and Lord of Scotland.

As the midsummer sun dipped behind the ridges of the Ochil Hills, a brief, grey gloaming crept down their southern slopes and edged across the land below. While the red-gold colours blazed behind the summits of King's Seat, the Law, Ben Cleuch, Blairdenon and Dumyat, updraughts carried eagles high into the blue of the night sky, the rays of the dying sun glowing russet on their wingspreads, tilting and swaying. As the great birds hunted, searching the heather and bracken for movement, fires twinkled and crackled on many hilltops. The Feast of the Nativity of the Baptist was also the solstice, the turning of the year, the beginning of summer, a time for farmers and their families to climb to the high places and light fires just as their ancestors had done since time out of mind. Even 1,314 years after the birth of Our Lord Jesus Christ, the old gods had not yet fled entirely and the needfires of midsummer licked into the night air to remember ancient beliefs.

At the western end of the Ochils, Dumyat was a fire-hill and also once a place of power. Its unusual name is from the Dun or Fortress of the Maeatae, an early Pictish kindred whose kings defied the might of Rome. In 208AD the warrior-emperor Septimius Severus marched north with a vast army of 40,000 legionaries and auxiliaries to destroy them and devastate their homelands.

It was and remains the largest army ever seen beyond the Tweed, but it failed to humble the Maeatae. The name of the western summit, Castle Law, recalls the defiance of the Pictish kings and the traces of their fort can still be clearly seen.

From the eastern summit of Dumyat proper, an immense vista opens to the south and east. In the half-dark of the night of 23 and 24 June 1314, those who gathered around the needfire will have been able to make out the distant glint of the River Forth as it looped and meandered across the flat carseland on its way to the widening horizon of the firth and the North Sea beyond. On the far side of the lazy river, the Roman road that brought the tramp of Severus' legions runs from the line of the Antonine Wall northwards past the foot of Dumyat to the outpost forts of the Gask Ridge and on to Bertha, Perth. In 208 and 1314, it was a vital artery, threading a way between the Forth and its marshy floodplain on one side and the wild hill country to the west.

Now marked on a modern map as the Gargunnock and Fintry Hills, the watershed ridges of the Carron Water and the Bannock Burn, this range of rolling hills across the waist of Scotland was seen as a frontier for many centuries. Known as Bannauc, it appears in the tale of the sixth-century wanderings of a mystical Welsh monk, St Cadoc, and in the roll of British Celtic warriors mustered for battle with the insurgent Angles in the south in 600AD, men came from 'beyond Bannauc'. Composed by the far-famed bard Aneurin in Edinburgh for the kings of the Gododdin, the epic poem sang of the rumble of war below Dumyat and the jingle of Dark Ages cavalry moving along the road by the Forth.

Legionaries and the warriors of half-forgotten kings passed below the glowering rock of Stirling. Singular and dramatic, it rises above the flat carseland like a sentinel. Flanked by the flood-plains to the east and the Bannauc and the treacherous Flanders Moss to the west, the fortress on the rock guarded the north road, the only road to Scotland beyond the Forth.

Watchers on the fire-hill of Dumyat could see something else, something that will have hollowed their bellies with fear. Far in the distance, they could make out the clustered pinpricks of hundreds of fires beyond the dark silhouette of Stirling Castle rock. None had been lit to celebrate the solstice. On either side of the Bannock Burn, as it slid through the carse towards the Forth, a vast army was attempting to make camp. Perhaps the echoes of thousands of voices, the shouts of sergeants, the creak and squeal of cartwheels and the shrieking neigh of horses carried as far as the dark heads of the hills.

Having marched more than 80 miles from Wark on the English side of the Tweed in only seven days, the soldiers of Edward II of England were exhausted, hungry and thirsty. Wearing full armour or the thick padded jackets and steel helmets of spearmen, they had sweated in the warmth of the midsummer sun and desperately needed to rest. The army had followed the metalled surface of the Roman road from Falkirk and the ruins of the old wall fort at Camelon but could not continue on to Stirling Castle. The way had been blocked by their enemies, the soldiers of the traitor, Robert Bruce, the usurper who claimed to be King of Scots. His dogged formations of spearmen had stood in their way.

Edward II and his commanders had been forced to wheel their huge, dispersed and unwieldy army to the east, towards the Forth, to a place where they could avoid the deep gorge of the Bannock Burn and cross at its lower reaches. Between it and the steep sides of the Pelstream Burn to the north, they reluctantly decided to make camp on what a later chronicler reckoned to be completely unsuitable ground.

Sir Thomas Grey's father had fought at Bannockburn and had passed on his vivid memories. In the *Scalachronica*, a history of the reigns of Edwards I, II and III, the Northumberland knight recorded an account of what happened and it carries the unmistakable ring of authenticity:

> The king's host left the [Roman] road through the woods and came to a plain in the direction of the River Forth, beyond Bannock Burn, an evil, deep marsh with streams, where the English troops unharnessed and remained all night in discomfort . . .

In the spring of 1314, the English king had sent out writs calling for the muster of an enormous, powerful force and had been answered with about 15,000 infantry and archers and approximately 2,500 armoured knights. At Wark and Berwick, soldiers had joined his host from England, Wales, Ireland, Gascony, France, Germany – and Scotland. Strung out in a long, vulnerable and slow-moving line on the Roman road, the army was not only exhausted but difficult to command effectively. When the vanguard of mounted knights reached the Bannock Burn, a column of infantry, archers and supply wagons stretched several miles behind them. The nature of the terrain and the tactics of the Scots king were already compressing them, compromising their tremendous superiority in numbers.

It appears that most of the heavy cavalry, the elite strike force of all large medieval armies, some archers and some infantry were able to cross the Bannock Burn late on Sunday evening, 23 June 1314. Much of Edward's expeditionary force, probably the bulk of the infantry, were left on the far side by the time the sun had dipped behind the Ochils. This would prove to be determinant. And if those who did succeed in crossing hoped to find a dry place for some much-needed rest, they were to be disappointed. Much work still needed to be done.

'The Bruce', John Barbour's poem in early Scots, was composed some considerable time after the battle but it relied on testimony from survivors. Here he describes the English army's attempt to make camp:

> They bivouacked there that night, down in the carse, and made every man clean and prepare his weapons and armour to be ready for battle in the morning. And because there were pows [sluggish streams] in the carse, they broke down houses and roofing and carried it off to make bridges by which to cross [the streams]. There are also some surviving who say that nearly all the men in the [Stirling] castle, knowing the difficulty the English army was in, came out after dark [about midnight], taking with them doors and windows. In this way the English had before daylight bridged the pows, so that everyone crossed over and had taken up a position on horseback on the hard field.

The makeshift bridges may have kept soldiers dry-shod but, as Barbour implies, their more important purpose was to safeguard Edward II's most effective and fearsome weapon, the English war-horses. Known as destriers, more than 2,000 had been led across the Bannock Burn in half-darkness to a restricted and treacherous terrain where at worst the heavy horses could have sunk to their hocks in cloying mud, or at best spooked and panicked if the earth seemed to suck at their hooves. And even well-trained horses will refuse to go near, far less cross, black water that seems to them bottomless. More problematic for knights and their squires was the fact that all warhorses used to be entire, stallions bred to be aggressive in the ruck of battle, biting and kicking out with their metal-shod hooves. Destriers were meant to be dangerous and corralling more than 2,000 in such a tight space was asking for trouble. And no doubt some men and animals were badly hurt before a blow had been struck in anger.

Throughout the short night, many of the destriers were kept bitted, harnessed and armoured. This made them easier to control but many will have pawed the mud-churned ground, knowing what wearing their war-gear meant, snorting, whinnying, itching for the gallop into the charge. Tense at the best of times, the atmosphere of the night before the morning will have been electric, and further charged by the reputation of the Scots for surprise attacks. Armed pickets will have been posted on the carse, peering into the gloaming, searching the edge of the treeline, the woods where the Scots were waiting.

Reserved and fenced on the instructions of King Alexander II in the mid thirteenth century, the New Park had been allowed to revert to a tangled wildwood. To give cover for deer and other prey, foresters had not managed the trees and undergrowth but let them seed, spread and thicken. It was also good cover for men, and King Robert Bruce knew that the park would protect his soldiers from cavalry and archers, the twin threats posed by the English army.

In what is known in Scots as the hindnight, when the midsummer sun had slid behind the Ochils to dim the carseland after midnight, the canopy of the trees made the tanglewood much darker, a place of shadows lit only by the campfires of Bruce's men. Having mustered his army at the Tor Wood, immediately to the south of the New Park, the king had reconnoitred the surrounding ground carefully and his men had been given time to set up camp in the shelter of the woods. And to prepare. Between 7,000 and 10,000 men had come to Stirling to fight. Most were infantry, spearmen who had the strength to wield long pikes in disciplined battlefield formations. There were archers, many of them from the Ettrick Forest, and about 500 light cavalry or skirmishers commanded by Sir Robert Keith. Scotland did not grow enough winter fodder to breed destriers and had not the wealth to afford squadrons of armoured knights.

Instead, Bruce and his commanders had probably summoned only chosen men, preferring them to those farmers, weavers and burgesses who joined a feudal host as an obligation. These were spearmen who would be resolute, who would remember their training in the heat and confusion of battle, men who would stand steady as the English roared their warhorses into the earth-shaking thunder of the charge. Men whom Bruce had often led.

Divided into four brigades, the Scots army had been marshalled into retreat order. From the muster at the Tor Wood, Thomas Randolph, Earl of Moray, had led the vanguard north up the Roman road into the New Park. He had been followed by two brigades commanded by Edward, the king's brother, and James Douglas. They halted in the midst of the park, facing the open carseland to the east. Bruce brought up the rearguard and stationed his men across the road at a place known as The Entry, where the old road cut through a stand of trees at the edge of the hunting reserve. Cautious, very unwilling to risk all he had achieved since 1307, the king had readied his army to march north or west and abandon Stirling Castle to the English. But he decided to wait, for the moment.

The days immediately before the Feast of St John the Baptist were dry and sunny and long. On the morning of Saturday, 22 June, lookouts almost certainly climbed the crumbling drystane walls of Tappoch Broch. Built some time around 500BC, its still substantial remains sat on a prominent hilltop in the Tor Wood that looked to the south-east, to where the English would come. Only four miles away stretched the line of the Antonine Wall and the grassy ruins of the forward fort at Camelon. From its ancient gateway the Roman road snaked north towards Bannockburn and Stirling Castle. The lookouts searched the southern horizon for the signs of the march of a vast army, perhaps a dust cloud, perhaps even the distant rumble of wagons and horsemen, almost certainly outriders scouting ahead.

Below the broch, captains had been shouting orders to their men to break camp, take up their weapons and fall into marching order. Bruce had mustered his host in the Tor Wood from late May onwards and now, as the front of battle loomed, they had withdrawn to his chosen deployment in the New Park, three miles to the north-west, moving up the Roman road, probably late in the morning. Meanwhile the lookouts on the broch sharpened their gaze to the south. No doubt Bruce's mounted scouts had galloped back with the news that Edward II's men were marching, having broken camp at Edinburgh early that Saturday morning.

With 20 miles to cover before they crossed the banks and ditches of the Antonine Wall and forded the River Carron at Camelon, the English must have set a brisk pace in the summer heat. It was a march forced by a timetable neither Bruce nor Edward II had set. A year before, the Scots king's impetuous brother, Edward, had agreed a truce with Sir Philip Moubray, the garrison commander of Stirling Castle. Although a Scot, he held Stirling for Edward of England, and it was one of the last strategic strongholds in enemy hands. Edward Bruce had laid a siege, an affair that was bound to be protracted since the Scots had few effective siege engines and the castle rock is even more forbidding and impressive than Edinburgh's. In addition, a waiting game did not suit the king's brother's hotheaded temperament and so, without consultation it seems, he concluded an agreement with Moubray. The Scots would withdraw – and use their forces more profitably elsewhere, Edward Bruce no doubt argued – on the condition that Moubray consented to surrender the castle if it was not relieved by an English army by midsummer 1314.

King Robert was apparently furious. His brother had virtually committed him to a pitched battle against what would unquestionably be a much larger force. And Moubray, perhaps more sensibly, had also committed the English king to an invasion. If Edward II's claim to be Lord of Scotland were to mean anything, then he would have to muster an army and march north before midsummer 1314. Bruce would then have a decision to make. Did he risk all on one encounter or did he retreat before the English king, scorching the earth and waiting for the invaders to starve, forcing them to turn back south? As the lookouts on the drystane walls of Tappoch Broch waited to see the flutter of English pennants on the horizon, the pieces set on the board in the summer of 1313 were at last moving, the great game was beginning. And the king of Scotland had not yet decided.

By the evening of Saturday, 22 June, the Scots army had settled down to bivouac under the trees of the New Park. Once cooking fires had been lit, pikes, axes, dirks and shields safely stowed near at hand and brackens pulled so that they could be laid down to soften the hard ground for a bed, the Scottish commanders met. Scouts had reported that Edward II had made camp at Falkirk, about 14 miles to the south-east. That intelligence set out a timetable and suggested a battle plan to Thomas Randolph, Earl of Moray, James Douglas, Edward Bruce, Walter Stewart, Aonghas Og MacDonald and their leader, Robert Bruce.

King Robert was an impressive, brave and regal figure. These adjectives were routinely attached in the flatteries of chroniclers, but in his case, they were probably no more than the truth. When Bruce's tomb was accidentally rediscovered at Dunfermline Abbey in the nineteenth century, the skeleton sealed in a lead coffin was that of a man who stood six foot, one inch tall. This contrasted with the average height of medieval Scotsmen at about five foot, six inches, and it made the king seem a giant to contemporaries. If Bruce's bearing was regal, even heroic, his attitudes almost certainly matched it. He came from a line of men who would be king.

Known as the Competitor, Robert Bruce, Lord of Annandale and grandfather of the king, contended all his long life for the throne of Scotland. When Alexander II was growing old and seemed unlikely to father an heir, the Great Council decided in 1238 that Bruce should succeed. He was of royal blood, directly descended from Earl Henry of Northumberland, the eldest son of David I. But the Competitor's hopes were thwarted when Alexander II remarried and his queen duly produced the future Alexander III. When the king's horse carried him to his death over the cliffs at Kinghorn in 1286, Robert Bruce competed once more, at the ripe age of 76. In 1292, he formally passed on his regal claims to his son and his heirs. And king at last, the Competitor's grandson believed absolutely in his right to rule, a confidence that never deserted him.

The Bruce, de Brus or de Bruis family probably originated in the Cotentin, the Cherbourg peninsula of north-western France and, like the Stewarts and others, Robert's ancestors arrived in Britain at the time of the Norman Conquest. A Scottish connection was soon established. In the early twelfth century David macMalcolm, the sixth son of King Malcolm Canmore, was forced to flee south to take refuge at the court of Henry I of England. The young Scot was raised in a thoroughly Anglo-Norman milieu and when his sister, Maud, married Henry to become queen of England, his status rose steeply. David was created Earl of Northampton, and then on the death of his brother, Alexander I, he unexpectedly succeeded to the throne of Scotland. Having forged personal and political relationships amongst the Anglo-Norman elite, David brought some of them north. The Bruces were given the lordship of Annandale and through marriage eventually became great landowners in the south-west of Scotland.

In England and Scotland the links forged between the men of the Norman elite were strong and they often transcended any fledgling sense of national loyalty. King Robert had relatives in the English army that had made camp on the night of 22 June at Falkirk, and old loyalties to others who would fight for Edward of England. Lords often changed sides in this and other medieval conflicts and those who fought alongside each other usually shared more than any notion of national attachment. Even as late as 1314 there was a powerful sense of a French-speaking Norman elite trading national loyalties in the furtherance of family fortunes.

Bruce and his captains were comrades in arms. Not only had they fought alongside each other through many campaigns and sieges, they had achieved much since King Robert was crowned at Scone in 1306. With patience and determination they had won back every important castle in Scotland, except Stirling. Perhaps Bruce's most accomplished soldier was also the least exalted. Until he was knighted before Bannockburn James Douglas held no title, yet his daring and ruthlessness did earn him something less formal – he was known as the Black Douglas. And for good reason.

In the winter darkness of Shrove Tuesday, the night of 19–20 February, Douglas led a remarkable assault on Roxburgh Castle, a huge fortress whose sparse ruins stand near Kelso, where the Teviot meets the Tweed. It is very formidable. Atop an oblong mound, partly man-made, its eastern flank slopes steeply to the banks of the Teviot and a weir built a little way upstream once diverted water into a moat that protected the equally precipitous western side. At the southern end the remains of a heavily defended gateway can still be clearly seen, while at the north end stood a barbican which was probably reached by a wooden bridge. This led out of the castle and into the streets of the town of Roxburgh, a prosperous marketplace for Borders wool. The burgh saw the beginning of urban life in early twelfth-century Scotland but now it has completely disappeared, not one stone stands upon another.

Under cover of the February darkness, Douglas and his men cloaked themselves carefully so that no glint of mail, armour or sword steel could be seen by the sentries on the ramparts. One fanciful account insists that the Black Douglas and his feral force disguised themselves as black cattle, crawling on all fours towards Roxburgh. Thoughtful as well as courageous, he planned the attack for the night of Shrove Tuesday because in the old sense of the term it was a carnival. Literally meaning a 'farewell to meat', a medieval carnival was held before the denials and privations of Lent and the date meant that most of the garrison of Roxburgh Castle would be in the great hall feasting and drinking. A few resentful sentries patrolled the wall walks, no doubt cocking an ear to the carousing, looking inwards not outwards, grumbling to themselves or perhaps even taking a sly bite or a consoling cup of something warming.

Below the walls, men who would spoil the party were edging ever closer. Douglas always tried to enlist local intelligence and as his men crept up the steep banks of the castle mount under their black cloaks, they were led by a Borderer, Sim of the Ledhouse. They carried an invention. Light and flexible rope ladders had been used by Bruce's captains since 1312 and the idea behind their design was simple. Men standing unobserved at the foot of a castle rampart could hoist the end of a rope ladder on the point of a long pike and attach a grappling hook onto the wall-head. It was usually quieter and more accurate than flinging a hinged hook over the defences. But at Roxburgh, the scrape of the grappling iron on the stonework brought a sentry running. He was quickly silenced by Sim of the Ledhouse, who 'stekit upward with ane knyff'. Scrambling over the ramparts, Douglas' men swarmed into Roxburgh, startling the men who were feasting and drinking, and achieving a tremendous triumph. Closest to the frontier with England, Roxburgh Castle was important to Edward II – and to the Scots. Once the castle had been secured, Douglas and his men did what they to slight the stone walls and towers in order to make the fortress difficult to defend if it were retaken by the English.

Thomas Randolph, Earl of Moray, commanded a brigade in Bruce's army and as he sat down with Douglas at the council of war in the shadows of the New Park, he could also reflect on a military triumph. Three weeks after the fall of Roxburgh, Moray's men broke into Edinburgh Castle in spectacular fashion. Again using the specialist knowledge of a local man, William Francis, he took an apparently impregnable stronghold from the English. Francis' father had been a soldier in the Edinburgh garrison and when the young William needed to sneak out unobserved to meet his girl in the town, astonishingly, he climbed down the near-sheer cliff-face of the castle rock. She must have been beautiful. But young Francis' youthful ardour helped conceive a plan.

While Moray's main force attacked the East Port of the mighty castle, still its only entrance, to create a diversion, William Francis led a group up the north face of the rock in darkness on the night of March 14th, 1314. Not only did these intrepid men climb successfully to the foot of Edinburgh's walls, they also carried the light rope ladders with them. Having pulled themselves up over the wall-head, they overpowered the sentries. And there must have been a substantial number of these extraordinary rock climbers because they raced to the East Port, attacked the defenders and got the gate open to let in Moray and his men.

None of these remarkable achievements would have been the subject of discussion between Bruce and his commanders as they talked in the circle of firelight under the trees of the New Park on the night of Saturday, 22 June. They sensed that their long and dogged campaign had come to its climax. The Scots army had been mustering in the Tor Wood for weeks and they will have ridden and walked the ground between it and Stirling more than once. They knew that in an open landscape with good ground for cavalry and room for archers that their spearmen would be thinned by volleys of arrows, outflanked, scattered and cut to pieces. The weight of numbers would tell. Instead it was better to choose and use the terrain to their advantage. One of the few positive elements of Edward Bruce's truce was that the Scots knew that the English had to march to Stirling and more, that there was only one route suitable for such a large army and its wagons and horses – the old Roman road. And where it entered the New Park, it might just be possible to gain a decisive advantage.

Such a stratagem had worked before. On 10 May 1307, Bruce chose to fight a much larger force of English cavalry and infantry at Loudoun Hill near Kilmarnock. Near the rocky knoll, he carefully chose ground where he could not be outflanked, rolled up and surrounded by a much more extended attack line of armoured knights. And then his men set to digging three sets of lateral trenches in front of their position, which they then covered over with branches and brackens. Led by the English governor of Scotland, Aymer de Valence, an army of 3,000 faced Bruce's 600 spearmen. They must have reckoned victory would be quick, but when the knights roared their destriers into the charge, peering through the slits in their steel visors, none could see what lay in their path. With lances couched and levelled, leaning forward in the saddle, the front rank of the English cavalry suddenly hit the trenches. More than 100 heavy horses went down in a moment, some catapulting fully armoured men into rotational falls, others screaming as their forelegs snapped. The second rank will have blundered into this appalling mêlée and those behind will have been pulling hard on their reins, swerving, skidding to avoid the churning mess of horseflesh and injured knights. To add to the murderous confusion, Bruce had left a narrow track open between the lateral ditches and as they slowed, hesitating as their comrades fell on either side, the few who reached the Scottish lines were beaten back as the spearmen advanced in formation.

At the New Park Bruce believed that he could achieve a similar effect and, no doubt at their council, his commanders agreed to set their men to work the following day. At The Entry, where the Roman road entered the trees of the New Park, pits or 'pots' were dug in what John Barbour described as a honeycomb pattern on either side of the metalled surface. Sharpened stakes were set in the bottom of each and the pots were then hidden just as the trenches had been at Loudoun Hill. In a twist of history, Roman soldiers had done something similar near at hand, 1,200 years before. To the north of the Antonine Wall, the direction from which trouble would come, they dug 'lilia' at Rough Castle, near Falkirk. There were ten rows of pots, offset, arranged like the black squares of a chessboard, and with sharpened stakes at the bottom of each one. They are still clearly visible.

Bruce's men left only the road untouched so that the English cavalry would be funnelled into a narrow front of only three or four mounted knights abreast at most. This sort of containment in a narrow space had worked well in 1297 at Stirling Bridge for William Wallace and Andrew Moray. And to limit English options ever further, all of the tracks through the New Park were closed off. Bruce then informed his council of war that his own brigade, the rearguard, would station themselves at The Entry. On the night before the morning, it seems that a limited action followed by a strategic withdrawal to the western hills may have been the consensus. But as the council of war ended and commanders returned through the woodland gloaming to their brigades, history began to stir.

2
The Muster

Vespers. The Feast of St Aurelian, the 16th day of June in the Year of Our Lord, 1314.

Towards the evening, the last of them breasted the rise at Barelees Rig and saw a sight that stopped even the hardest of their hearts. On the flat haugh-land by the banks of the River Tweed almost 18,000 men had answered the king's summons and marched and ridden to the muster at Wark. The last to come saw a vast military camp sprawling westwards along the banks of the great river for more than four miles. Perched on a kaim in the midst of a myriad of pavilions, awnings, corrals, ox-carts and cooking fires stood Wark Castle and the latecomers could see the royal standards flying from the battlements of its squat little keep. The fortress had been built on the natural mound of the kaim as a motte and bailey by the Norman lord Walter Espec in the early twelfth century and it looked north over the Tweed to a wide panorama of a different country. The river marked the eastern frontier between the realms of England and Scotland, and watchers at Wark could see for many miles over the fertile farmlands of the Merse of Berwickshire, enemy territory.

It was not the first time that those who farmed the fertile fields by the banks of the Tweed had seen an English army make camp. Edward I had mustered an invasion force in the fields below Wark in 1296 and again in 1300 his household set up a royal court in the tower. Not only did it stand glowering at Scotland like a frontier guard, its courtyard, the old bailey, stretched down to the Tweed where there were reliable fords for an army and its wagons to splash across. Small river-islands known as *annas* made the passage easier. All that remains of Wark Castle now is a string of steep grassy humps by the roadside, but history swirled around these buried, tumble-down walls for at least half a millennium. And in the summer of 1314 the old fortress once more stood in the midst of British politics.

Medieval hosts mustered only in the summer – when the grass grew. Over the broad haughland below Wark between 8,000 and 10,000 animals were grazing. Armoured knights had brought their snorting destriers, at least 2,500 of them, and as many coursers or riding horses. Squires and sergeants who served them rode palfreys, probably ponies, and smaller gelded horses known as hackneys. Sumpters and mules pulled lighter carts of general supplies, military equipment, thousands of sheaves of arrows, crossbow bolts, even furniture. Ox-cart teams of four beasts yoked together pulled heavier loads, items such as portable cornmills, thousands of horseshoes, anvils and bulk supplies of food such as corn. Herds of cattle and flocks of sheep were driven to the haughland at Wark as a mobile supply of food. All of these arrivals will have progressively stripped the ground of its spring grass, nibbling it down to the roots. The muster was late, time wore on towards midsummer and the fields of Wark could not sustain such a vast army for long.

As important as grass was water, and several streams join the Tweed, running through the pasture where animals were corralled or tethered. And below Wark Castle the banks of the river become much less precipitous towards the east. Grooms and herdsmen will have led their beasts down to the waterside several times each day. The ground ridges abruptly south of the flat haugh and while sheep, cattle and even oxen will have been moved up onto Wark Common to relieve the pressure on grazing, the precious destriers and coursers stayed near the Tweed.

Roman camps have been found near Wark and their locations imply a lost road. Almost all who came to the muster approached from the south-east, coming up the Milfield Plain. In the first or second centuries AD, a marching camp was dug by the legions at East Learmouth, and in 1826 and 1827, a cache of hundreds of Roman coins was discovered nearby at Camp Hill, an Iron Age fortress of the first millennium BC. Another Roman marching camp was made at Carham, two miles west of Wark. The modern roads across the plain and along the south bank of the Tweed mostly run arrow-straight and may cover the course of the old metalled surface laid down by the legionaries and their engineers, much of which probably survived into the early fourteenth century.

Show mattered in medieval armies and when noblemen arrived at the muster at Wark, they will have come in all their finery. Lords wore surcoats over their mail and armour and their destriers were dressed in caparisons, decorated protective coverings blazoned with arms, the three golden lions on a red ground being the most famous, the arms of King Edward II. When he arrived at Wark, trumpets announced a great retinue of 89 household knights in embroidered silk surcoats with caparisons moving with the stride of their destriers, and 32 bannerets, lords who commanded detachments of men who rode and marched under their own flag. In the sunshine of June 1314, the fields of Wark were fields of dreams, dreams of glory at Stirling.

There were notable absentees, a consequence of a cruelly

divided court and the behaviour of a king who could not command the support and respect of most of his great magnates. Piers Gaveston was the cause, and his spectre would come north to haunt the battlefield at Bannockburn. The son of a Gascon nobleman, he appears to have been striking-looking, the picture of chivalry and very proficient in the knightly arts of war. First noticed by Edward I some time around 1305, the young man was attached to the household of the heir to the throne, Edward of Caernarvon, as he then was. The two men almost certainly became lovers.

When in 1306/7 the old king marched north once more and halted his army at Lanercost Priory, not far from Carlisle, he discovered that his son was planning to award Gaveston one of the many lucrative lordships belonging to the royal family. The Gascon would become the Count of Ponthieu in Picardy, in northern France. Enraged by this, Edward I attacked his son at Lanercost, tearing out lumps of his hair in front of startled courtiers. But this bout of royal fury only served to galvanise Edward in his determination to advance his lover. When the English army moved north and turned west along the line of Hadrian's Wall to Burgh by Sands on the southern shores of the Solway Firth to begin the crossing to Scotland (because of the treacherous ground of the Solway Moss to the west, armies preferred to wade across the fords at low tide, coming ashore on the Scottish side at the prehistoric stone circle around the Lochmaben Stane, a clear seamark), Edward I's famous constitution at last broke down and the Hammer of the Scots died before he could lead a last expedition to tame the north. Proclaimed king at Burgh, Edward II wasted no time and conferred the earldom of Cornwall on Gaveston. His magnates shook their heads. It was not a good beginning.

What appalled the earls of Lancaster, Warwick, Lincoln and the other great landowners was not that their king had taken a man for his lover. There were plenty of precedents, that predilection did not preclude the production of heirs, heroes of Rome and Greece had been homosexuals and in any case what went on in the royal bedchamber was far less important than what happened in the council chamber. But gossip whispered its way around the royal court, and at Edward II's coronation the muttering grew louder as a chronicler reported that the 'familiaris', the favourite, 'was so decked out that he more resembled the god Mars than an ordinary mortal'.

In a royal or otherwise autocratic form of government, access to the autocrat is crucial. And such was Gaveston's hold over the king that he controlled access and influence. The writer of the *Life of Edward II* noted 'Piers alone received a gracious welcome from the king, and the king would speak to no one save in his presence'. Worse, this Gascon upstart was insulting. Because he was tall and had a pale complexion, the Earl of Pembroke, Aymer de Valence, was nicknamed 'Joseph the Jew' by the royal favourite. The Earl of Lincoln was 'old burst-belly', and Gloucester no better than a 'whoreson'. The ill-feeling caused by the cruel and extravagant insults was exacerbated by Gaveston's skill in tournaments and jousts. These formal occasions could result in injury, even death, but none of the great magnates he so roundly derided could defeat the picture of chivalry in the lists. The ghost of Piers Gaveston would come to fight on the battlefield at Bannockburn – on the side of the Scots.

Simmering residual tension ensured that only three earls joined the muster at Wark. Gloucester, Pembroke and Hereford had ridden north with their retinues but more of England's most powerful landowners had pointedly made excuses and not stirred from their castles. Thomas, Earl of Lancaster, was of royal descent on both sides of his family tree, held five earldoms and was enormously wealthy. But he and Edward II loathed each other. Lancaster sent to the muster only the bare minimum number of men his rank obliged him to. Guy Beauchamp, Earl of Warwick, and the Earl of Lincoln, 'old burst-belly', were also notable absentees. In 1313 all had nominally made peace with their king, having been complicit in the murder of Piers Gaveston a year before. He had been abducted and imprisoned in Scarborough Castle and, probably at the behest of Warwick, the royal favourite had been taken out of the gates by two Welsh soldiers and some way along a road, out of the sight of onlookers. There the Welshmen ran him through with their swords before hacking off his head. Edward II was devastated, desolated and incandescent with rage. Never reconciled to Lancaster, the king was probably relieved that England's most powerful magnate had not come to Wark, but the absence of five earls did not say much for support for royal policy and unity of purpose.

Almost certainly inside the walls of Wark Castle, and since witness was important, in front of a gathering of noblemen who had come north to fight, Edward II distributed the promised fruits of the inevitable victory to come. The estates of the opposing Scottish commanders were parcelled out and the earldom of Moray, the lands of Thomas Randolph, were awarded to Hugh Despenser. The earldom was a rich prize and a clear signal to all who attended the king that day at Wark that a new favourite had been installed in Piers Gaveston's place. So confident of success and the gift of Moray was Despenser that his baggage wagons carried furniture and tapestries to make his new halls in Scotland more homely. The fact that he must have known in advance of the gathering at Wark that he was to be given Moray says much about how close Despenser and the king had become. It was as though Edward II had learned nothing from his destructive affair with Gaveston, as though he was careless of how his sexual appetites might come to prejudice the success of his policy and the vast expedition brought together to conquer Scotland.

When Edward doled out his list of Scottish prizes, he will have done it in French, the language of the English court until the end of the fourteenth century, when Richard II was the first king to prefer English. The fields around Wark Castle rang with many languages; sergeants roared orders to infantrymen in English, knights spoke to their squires in French (and German, for there were knights who had crossed the seas to fight for Edward for a fee and the promise of plunder) and for men who had approached the muster from the north and the west, their commanders spoke to some of them in Scots. In 1306 Robert Bruce had famously murdered his rival, John Comyn, at the altar of the Greyfriars Kirk in Dumfries. That desecration had propelled Bruce into insurrection and eventually to his crowning a year later. The Comyns remained his sworn enemies and they brought men to fight alongside the English. No doubt Edward promised them land. And the Comyns were not alone. Enemies of Clan Donald and their chief, Aonghas Og, who was in the New Park with Bruce at Stirling, the MacDougalls and the MacNabs had come to Wark with warriors, men with axes, mail-shirts and Gaelic in their mouths.

They were not the most numerous speakers of a Celtic language at the muster. Five thousand Welshmen, many of them summoned by the Earl of Hereford, had made the long journey north with their spears and their longbows. And the Scots feared archers. With their rapid firepower and tremendous upper body strength, companies of archers could send death whooshing into the sky above formations of spearmen. Like a bombardment of modern artillery softening up a target, the loosing of thousands of arrows was a murderous prelude to the charge of the armoured knights. Spearmen could not afford the armour needed to protect against the hail of arrows falling amongst them, their aketons, padded jackets, would easily be pierced and shields turned to the skies left fatal gaps. The Welsh and English archers at Wark did not indulge in the show and dash of their knightly comrades and their prancing destriers, but they would win the battle and glory for them if the wind did not blow and the ground was good and open.

Before his arrival at the muster Edward II had been in Berwick. The most prosperous town in twelfth-century Scotland, its harbour was the point of export for the Borders wool crop. Having bargained over the size and quality of the woolpacks at the inland market at Roxburgh, Flemish, Italian and English merchants had them transported down the Tweed, perhaps by raft, more likely by a well-known *via regis*, King's Road. It ran on the north bank of the river. The documents associated with Kelso Abbey spoke of the 'road used by the abbot's carts' on their way to Berwick. The port had prospered off the backs of Border sheep and such was the volume and importance of the trade that European merchants had set up trading halls behind Berwick's walls. They were also keeping secure stockpiles of grain that had been arriving for weeks. An Italian banker, Antonio Pessagno, had lent the king £21,000 to buy most of it and 60 ships had been commandeered to take on board these vital stores at Berwick's quays. They would then sail out of the mouth of the Tweed and set a course up the Scottish coastline to drop anchor in Leith Roads, or perhaps off Cramond, to rendezvous with the invading army as it moved down off the Lammermuir Hills.

Ill-judged in his choice of favourites and reckless with his patronage he most certainly was, but apparently Edward II was possessed of great physical courage. Tall like Bruce, he was also accounted athletic and strong. And he readily recognised the fighting qualities of others. According to John Barbour, Sir Giles d'Argentan was reckoned to be 'the third best knight of his day' (Henry, the Holy Roman Emperor, and Robert Bruce were ranked first and second), and Edward exerted himself greatly to bring him to Wark. Captured on the island of Rhodes, probably while fighting as a mercenary, d'Argentan had been imprisoned at the Greek city of Salonika, part of the Byzantine Empire. Between August and October 1313, Edward II had no fewer than 11 letters written to, amongst others, the Podesta of Genoa, an Italian city-state with several possessions in the Aegean Sea (and possibly d'Argentan's employer), to the Holy Roman Emperor, Henry, and to both the Emperor and Empress of Byzantium pleading for the release of the great knight. Sir Giles had fought in the victory at Falkirk over the forces of William Wallace, and the English king judged that his presence in Scotland in 1314 would add strength and morale.

When D'Argentan rode across the flat pastureland below Wark Castle, he saw something that was second nature to knights like himself: many groups of men and horses working together. Destriers were not simply a means of delivering an armoured knight and his lance or sword to a point of impact. Riders and warhorses needed to fight as a unit and to understand each other perfectly. A misunderstood aid or command or the inability of a horse to fiddle its feet at precisely the right moment could mean the difference between life and death – for both. In the murderous mêlée of battle, horse and rider needed to turn, advance, swerve or pull back in seconds so that blows could be delivered or avoided. And both of them needed to be able to fight.

A battle scene from the Holkham Picture Bible illustrates well what went on, how the knights and horses that mustered at Wark went about the business of war. It was savage. As the mounted men stab with their lances and swing their swords and axes, the destriers bite and kick out their metal-shod hooves. The thick, heavy war horseshoes and big clench-nails are clearly depicted in the Holkham Bible. And knights attack horses as well as each other. One has driven his lance through a destrier's neck to skewer its rider as it is about to rear and throw him. At the foot of the picture dying horses thrash their hooves and bite at the feet of those riding them down. And perhaps appropriately or coincidentally, a king is shown cleaving through a knight's helm with an axe.

By any modern measure, these men were superb horsemen. Training began young at the age of seven. Known as pages, the first and most important phase of instruction for these boys was concerned with the care of horses, how to look after these great beasts, how to groom them, what feeds were best and appropriate (before battle, destriers were probably given 'heating' buckets of corn or warm mash to fire them up), how to put on harness properly, what bits worked best and much else. These were all stallions and they could be aggressive and difficult to manage. Such is their size and strength, no horse can be forced to do anything it does not acquiesce in. Pages needed to be taught what aids to use and when, how to persuade a horse to move with the use of the reins, legs, feet and seat. And crucially, how to ride with the reins in only one hand so that the other could wield a weapon, or how to ride and fight having dropped the reins on their horse's neck.

At about the age of 14 a page became a squire as he was assigned to a knight. Training with weapons and armour began and to improve riding skills, hunting was seen as useful as well as entertaining. Royal forests and parks like the New Park at Stirling had a military function as well as a role in stocking the larder. The pursuit of a dodging and weaving deer taught boys how to sit tight and gallop through woodland and how to duck and sway to avoid low branches.

As contingents waited for the muster at Wark to complete, pages and squires used the time to prepare and maintain equipment. Made from thousands of rings of steel a little larger than a wedding ring, mail shirts were the basic protection worn by mounted knights. Some could also afford plate armour to cover some or all of it. Already very heavy, these items were worn over a padded coat. Helms were also padded inside with hay, wool or tow and they needed to fit precisely so that the eye-slit lined up with the wearer's eyes. Knights could be rendered blind, and probably dead if a helm slipped back or forward. Helms were also hot, and sweat could sting and impair vision. Some men preferred to wear kettle helms. Only covering the head and not the face, they looked a little like a broader-brimmed version of the tin hats of World War Two. Kettle helms did not restrict vision and were cooler but their wearers would have their faces more readily stabbed at.

All riders wore spurs, and if their destriers wore chain mail under their caparisons, they will have to have been sharp to make any impression. Swords were the symbolic as well as the preferred weapons. Knights were knighted with them (they still are) and they were central to the elaborate ceremonies of chivalry. But lances were thought to be extremely effective in battle when squadrons of knights fought in formation. In what must have been an awesome sight, especially for an enemy opposite, a charge began with men closing up their ranks so that they began at a walk, knee to knee. As they drew nearer, the line broke into a trot, then a canter and at the last moment into a galloping charge. Only then were lances levelled and war cries roared.

Before he reached Wark, Edward II knew where Bruce had deployed. From Newminster near Morpeth, he sent a dispatch on 27 May which noted that 'the Scots are striving to assemble great numbers of foot in strong and marshy places, extremely hard for cavalry to penetrate, between us and our castle of Stirling'. And at Wark, 20 days later, Edward knew that time was running out. To relieve his castle, he had to lead his vast army there before midsummer, 24 June. Feverish activity began as wagons were loaded, animals herded, horses harnessed and infantry stood to. And on 17 June 1314, on the day after the Feast of St Aurelian, the English army splashed across the fords at Wark and entered the realm of Scotland.

3
The Tor Wood

May, the Year of Our Lord, 1314, the eighth year of the reign of Robert, the first of that name, by the grace of God, King of Scotland.

Size and length mattered to Robert Bruce and his spearmen. If a mounted knight's lance projected six feet beyond the head of his charging destrier, then a pike held by a Scottish spearman had to be long enough to keep the enemy lance point from reaching his chest. That meant a very long shaft of nine or even twelve feet, and a very strong man to wield it. Like archers, spearmen needed tremendous upper body strength and the ability to control and direct the business end of a pike that would extend a long way in front him, the principle of levers operating in reverse. And these men were also required to be athletic. Where and how the holder of a pike placed his feet and braced himself for impact was vital. If he even made contact with a charging knight or his destrier, their momentum would be much greater and could knock him backwards with ease. Men who stood in the front rank often kneeled so that they could couch the butt-end of their pikes in the ground. Also vital was a spearman's ability to move smartly in concert with his comrades, just in the manner demanded by King Robert and his captains. As the Scottish army mustered amongst the May blossom in the Tor Wood, infantry soldiers, their drill sergeants and their commanders began to train for the battle that was approaching up the old road.

Politics, ambition and the green shoots of nationhood had

brought Robert Bruce and his men to the Tor Wood, to a midsummer date that would settle destinies. But mysticism and prophecy had also played a part in the unfolding drama, a part modern sensibilities often underestimate. The prophet was True Thomas, Thomas the Rhymer, Thomas of Ercildoune, a man who would become famous across Britain and much of medieval Europe. Many believed that what True Thomas prophesied came to pass, and it seemed to all who heard tell of his words that he could reach back into a past beyond the time of the saints and Holy Mother Church, to a past when men could understand the minds of the old Celtic gods and how they ordained the future.

Robert Bruce claimed kingship of many Scotlands. To the north and west of the Highland Boundary Fault that runs so abruptly from Stonehaven on the North Sea coast to Glasgow and the Clyde, Gaelic was spoken and the kinship of the clans was forming. The great Atlantic principality of the Lords of the Isles had been a force for stability since the middle of the twelfth century, the time of Somerled the Viking. And in the south-west, in Galloway, the land of the Gall-Gaidheil, the Stranger-Gaels, another dialect of Gaelic was heard. As Earl of Carrick and Lord of Annandale, Bruce certainly spoke Gaelic, the language of his mother, Marjorie of Galloway, and of the majority of the tenants of his earldom, his power-base in the west. By contrast, Annandale had been settled by farmers who spoke early Scots and perhaps even Norse. Place-names such as Criffel (Kraka Fjall, the Raven Fell) and Tinwald (the place where a 'thing' or a Norse-style legislature met) recall the language the Vikings brought to the Solway shore. Along the fertile Moray coastlands, the Angus and Tayside plains, Fife, the Lothians, the western end of the Midland Valley and in the Tweed Valley, Scots was widely spoken. But not everywhere.

North of the Tweed and its prosperous, towering abbeys at Melrose, Jedburgh, Dryburgh and Kelso, in the hills above Lauderdale and Gala Water, the old language was still spoken, the oldest language to describe Scotland. In remote farmsteads in the valleys of the Heriot Water, Soonhope, Earnscleuch, Blythe and in many other isolated places, people spoke of their daily lives, the landscape, the weather and the future in a northern dialect of Old Welsh, the Celtic tongue spoken all over Britain when the Romans came 13 centuries before. Place-names mark the word 'tref' for a settlement in metathetical versions along the Gala Water at Torsonce and Torquhan and other Old Welsh names sprinkle the map at Peebles, Kelso and Penicuik.

True Thomas knew this ancient speech and it is likely that much of his poetry and prophesy came from listening at winter firesides in the Border hills. A bard and a seer, he was a thoroughly Celtic figure and because they were widely believed, his visions became part of Scotland's story. None more than what he foretold on 19 March 1286. Thomas Rhymer had been summoned to the hall of the man who was probably his patron, the Earl of Dunbar. He held a castle in Earlston in Lauderdale. His name was Patrick, in itself a memory of the Celtic past in Lowland Scotland for it was borne by his seven forebears as earl. The first of them used the full version of Gospatrick and it comes from the Old Welsh, Gwas Padraig, the Servant of St Patrick.

No doubt the fire roared in the earl's hall as ale and wine were passed around his retinue, many of them fighting men. Once all had settled, entertainment was needed and Patrick asked his bard, True Thomas, what prophecies he had. Even across six centuries, there is a hint of derision, even scepticism. This was what Walter Bower recorded in the annals of the *Scotichronicon*:

> The earl had asked him, half-jesting as usual, what news the next day would bring. Thomas gave a sobbing sigh from the depths of his heart, and is said to have made this clear pronouncement to the earl in front of his retainers:
>
> 'Alas for tomorrow, a day of calamity and misery! Because before the stroke of twelve a strong wind will be heard in Scotland the like of which has not been known since times long ago. Indeed its blast will dumbfound the nations and render senseless those who hear it; it will humble what is lofty and raze what is unbending to the ground.'

The same day Thomas stunned the men in Dunbar's castle in Earlston into open-mouthed silence, more men were feasting 40 miles to the north. At Edinburgh Castle King Alexander III and some of his great magnates and members of the royal council had probably been enjoying some Gascon wine for in the afternoon the talk turned to appetites of another kind. The king's new and young wife, Yolande de Dreux, was at his manor in Kinghorn, 20 miles away in Fife, across the Firth of Forth. No matter that the afternoon was growing dark and the weather was foul, the wind whipping spindrift off the firth, the king would see his beautiful wife – that very day! It was his royal duty, was it not, to father an heir to the throne? Fuelled by wine or not, this was a more than usually pressing issue. The king was right! There was no male heir in direct line of succession. Alexander's two sons had died before him and all that would carry on the royal blood of the macMalcolm dynasty was a granddaughter, Margaret, the little Maid of Norway. And so it was vital that the king braved the elements to bed his young wife. As soon as possible! And despite much discouragement, Alexander had his horse saddled and with only three squires as an escort, clattered over the cobbles out of Edinburgh Castle to ride for Dalmeny and the Forth ferry. It was a headstrong, impulsive decision, one that would cost Scotland very dear, one that would turn the course of history.

When the king reached the shore at Dalmeny, it was late in the day, growing very dark, the wind howled across the firth and it may also have been raining. At first the ferryman refused to go out in such weather, even if it was his king demanding to cross. Asked if it was because he was afraid, he replied nobly and perhaps apocryphally, 'I could not die better than in the company of your father's son.' No doubt more than one coin was passed over. Lookouts at Inverkeithing must have been astonished to see a rowing boat bobbing on the swell, for when Alexander and his squires scrambled ashore they were met by one of the burgesses of the town. Known to the king, Alexander Le Saucier was a maker of sauces in the royal kitchens and he addressed his royal master with an attractive directness that seems to have become characteristic for all Scots, no matter their social status. It was now black-dark on a stormy late winter's evening, and after his offer of a bed for the night was rejected by the king, le Saucier scolded him like a child; 'My lord, what are you doing out in such weather and darkness? How many times have I tried to persuade you that midnight travelling will bring you no good?'

Alexander III's ardour had not been dampened by the storm and he insisted on riding the few miles to Kinghorn and his wife's bed. With two local men to guide him, he and his squires disappeared into the darkness. And not long after they left Inverkeithing, the king disappeared from history. He was never seen alive again.

Perhaps spooking at the wind or losing its footing on the shore path, Alexander's horse fell and pitched its rider over the steep and rocky cliffs at Pettycur. On the morning after the storm, the king's body was found on the beach. His neck had been broken. And a much greater storm was about to burst over Scotland.

The terrible news travelled fast, quickly reaching Earlston. Here is Walter Bower again:

> Because of his [True Thomas] grave words the earl and his retainers kept watch over the next day, carefully observing the passing of the hours until noon. Seeing no clouds or signs of wind in the sky, they decided that Thomas was out of his mind and hurried off to dinner. The earl had scarcely sat down at the table and the hand of the clock was almost at midday when the earl's ears were smitten with the importunate knocking of someone who had arrived at the gate demanding to be admitted into his presence immediately. So the stranger was let in and asked for his news. 'News I have,' he said, 'but it is bad news which will reduce the whole realm of Scotland to tears – because alas! Its noble king met the end of his life on earth at Kinghorn last night. And this is what I have come to tell you.' At this news the earl and all his household, as if awaked from a deep sleep, beat their breasts. They discovered by experience that the prophecies of the said Thomas had become all too credible.

When Margaret, the Maid of Norway, died in 1290, the direct line of the macMalcolm kings was ended and their kingdom began a long period of turmoil and trial. The competing claims of Edward I of England and what came to be called the Community of the Realm of Scotland turned on the principle of homage, and the legal battle lines had been drawn a few decades before. On 29 October 1278, at Westminster, Alexander III had formally agreed that he was a vassal of Edward, but only for those estates that he held in England. 'I become your man for the lands I hold of you in the kingdom of England for which I owe homage, saving my kingdom.' Immediately, there was an objection. William Middleton, the Bishop of Norwich, asserted; 'And be it saved to the king of England if he have a right to homage for it?' Alexander would have none of it. 'No one has a right to homage for my kingdom of Scotland save God alone, and I hold it only of God.' For almost half a century, the history of Scotland – and England – would turn on this argument.

After the death of the little Maid of Norway and the extinction of the direct macMalcolm line, Robert Bruce and John Balliol pressed their claims to the throne, and the danger of civil war presented itself. The Competitor and Balliol were both of undoubted royal descent, both wealthy and well-landed, and both capable of raising armies of supporters quickly. At the invitation of Bishop Fraser of St Andrews, Edward I of England adopted the role of adjudicator and a joint session of the parliaments of Scotland and England was uniquely convened at Norham, where there stood a formidable castle on the English bank of the Tweed built by the prince-bishops of Durham, not far from Wark. The only building large enough to accommodate this joint session of parliament was the Norman church in the village.

Characteristically, Edward I seized the opportunity to assert what Alexander III had denied him. 'Can you produce any evidence to show that I am not the rightful suzerain of Scotland?' was the question the king's lawyers had formulated. And it was of course heavily loaded. Edward gave the Scots three weeks to answer, a very short time. In the event a letter written in French supplied a brilliantly measured response. 'In the name of the Community of the Realm of Scotland' it stated that the suzerainty or overlordship of the nation was an issue that could be decided only if a Scottish king existed to decide it. What a parliament or its commissioners might believe or pronounce was irrelevant. Here is Bower again:

> Robert Wishart, Bishop of Glasgow, briefly replied that from long ago the kingdom of Scotland was free to the extent that it owed tribute or homage to no one save God alone and his agent on earth; and he added to the aforesaid these words which I shall record: 'Your majesty, I have made extracts from the books of the English, namely a prophecy of Gildas, as follows:
>
> The kingdom of the Scots was once noble, strong and powerful
> Among the other kingdoms of the earth.
> After repelling the Britons, Norwegians, Picts and Danes,
> The Scots nobly upheld their rights.
>
> On hearing this the king passed over the bishop's reply with a deaf ear as if deeming it worthless, and planned to proceed further and insist with all his strength on a new regime in the kingdom. He

> refrained from further reference to his own claim, and after taking advice privately, entreated the prelates, magnates and nobles of Scotland to come to Berwick and there (such was his offer) have their case decided in a trustworthy manner.

Edward believed that the letter was equally irrelevant to his aims and it is clear from Bower that whatever cover the legalisms of feudal relationships might offer, the English overlordship of Scotland would be driven through. And when Bruce, Balliol and the magnates and prelates met at Berwick Castle, a deal was going to be done, no matter what the arguments were. Bower makes that clear:

> After quickly deliberating with his advisors (who had been quite corrupted), Balliol agreed to the aforesaid king's wish that he should hold the kingdom of him and do homage for the same. When this had been done, the parties [Bruce and Balliol] were summoned into the presence of the nobles of Scotland and England, and Edward declared John de Balliol to be the lawful heir in succession to the kingdom and adjudged him to have the better right.

Robert Bruce left Berwick immediately and never did homage to Balliol. From the outset it was a difficult and ultimately humiliating kingship, scarcely worth the name. King John duly swore homage to Edward I for Scotland and this allowed litigants to appeal over his head to the English king as the feudal superior. Balliol was forced to appear in front of the English parliament and admit his fault in these cases. It must have been excruciating. This was followed by a demand that King John and his great magnates should join Edward I's feudal host to fight in France. Pressure in Scotland built and quickly boiled over in 1295 when a council of 12 earls effectively took power out of King John's hands. At Montrose a year later he was publically stripped of kingship and Edward I was said to have commented that 'a man does good business when he rids himself of a turd'. Battle lines were being drawn all across the nation and the war for Scotland was beginning.

In an affray in May 1296, William Wallace killed the English sheriff of Lanark. It sparked rebellion and momentum. At the same time Andrew Moray led an attack on the English garrison at Inverness. Both leaders attracted the support of powerful and disaffected magnates: the earls of Fife and Buchan, and the grandson of the Competitor, Robert Bruce, the Earl of Carrick. A dramatic victory was won at Stirling Bridge in 1297. It was to be a heroic but brief flicker. After the death of Moray from wounds suffered at Stirling, Wallace became Guardian of the Realm in the name of King John, a prisoner in the Tower of London. A year later, Edward I led an army of 12,000 men north and at Falkirk, on open ground, defeated the Scots with a deadly combination of archers and the charge of armoured knights. Wallace fled into hiding and over the next eight years the English tightened their grip on Scotland, taking and garrisoning strategic castles.

Robert Bruce's response to the failure of William Wallace and the determination of Edward I to bring Scotland firmly under his control was direct. He deserted. In 1302, Bruce abandoned the patriotic party and in the phrase of the times, came into the English king's peace. His reasoning was unblushing: Bruce believed that Edward I would support his claim to the Scottish throne. Simple as that.

Anachronistic attitudes often skew perceptions of the past and even the phrase 'the patriotic party' is almost inappropriate. For the elite, personal and family advantage rather than patriotism is what drove decision-making in the early fourteenth century, just as it usually does in the early twenty-first. Farmers and burgesses may have fervently wished to see the end of the colonial regime of English occupation when it shaded into violence and exploitation, but native lords could also behave badly towards their social inferiors. Like the English royal family, the English and Scottish magnates and most of the influential prelates, Robert Bruce was of Norman descent and his first loyalty was to his family and its interests. A century before, the chronicler Walter of Coventry commented: 'The modern kings of Scotland count themselves as Frenchmen, in race, manners, language and culture; they keep only Frenchmen in their household and following, and have reduced the Scots to utter servitude'. This is exaggerated but it does express a central truth. These families saw themselves as a race apart, even if the differences will have diluted in the time between the reign of William the Lion and John Balliol.

Certainly there were actions and statements made in the course of the Wars of Independence that suggest the growth of what might be called national sentiment, as opposed to family interest – and Bruce was not above playing on that. For someone who claimed the kingship of Scotland, it was no more than appropriate to assert a different identity and history. But like John Balliol, Bruce seemed willing to see that subsumed under English control and it appears that he was willing to do homage to Edward

I to secure the crown. In 1302 his father, also Robert Bruce, was living on the family's English estates and he had done homage to the English king.

At the same time as Bruce was making his way south to the royal court, probably at the Tower of London, a momentous battle was fought in Flanders. At issue was Flemish independence from France. Armed with long spears or pikes called geldons, an army of farmers and burgesses formed up in massed formations on ground that was boggy and crossed by streams, and defeated squadrons of French armoured knights. It was the first time a force of pikemen had ever beaten back medieval Europe's most powerful military elite. Courtrai must have stayed in the minds of strategists for at least a generation.

Two years later Robert Bruce concluded what became known as the Cambuskenneth Compact with William Lamberton, Bishop of St Andrews. The stimulus was probably the death of Bruce's father. Including the interesting comfort-phrase, 'that neither of them should undertake any important business without the other of them', the compact was agreed at the siege of Stirling Castle, where Bruce and his men were part of the English army. There was also a clear but unwritten understanding that when Edward I died – he was 66 – Bruce would then become king of Scotland. Hopes were raised a year later when the English king grew gravely ill and was not expected to live. According to John Barbour, an enthusiastic supporter of Bruce, another deal was made.

John Comyn, Earl of Buchan, was also of Norman descent and his family had gained the rank of earl before the Bruces. Although he and Robert had been joint Guardians of the Realm before 1302, their partnership had not been amicable. Their mutual dislike had even escalated to violence and they had come to blows. But as Edward I supposedly lay dying and glittering prizes beckoned, old enmities were suppressed. The deal was a simple exchange. If Comyn supported Bruce for the crown, he would receive all of the Bruce family's wide estates in the south-west and elsewhere, and if on the other hand Bruce supported Comyn for the kingship then all of the Comyn lands in the north would go to Bruce. Which was it to be? Barbour reported that Comyn chose the land rather than the throne and in a signed document agreed to back Bruce's royal ambitions.

But Edward I inconveniently recovered. And to Comyn it seemed that all bets were off. In fact the agreement might be turned to his advantage. The old warrior king was beginning to suspect Bruce's loyalty and when John Comyn whispered behind his hand that treason had been plotted, Edward nodded and decided to have the Earl of Carrick arrested.

Routinely brutal and utterly ruthless, the English king would have convened a court of peers in the Tower of London and instructed a guilty verdict. In turn that would have brought in its wake the horrific death of a traitor. Like William Wallace only a few months before, Bruce would have been stripped naked in the Tower, tied to a hurdle harnessed to a horse and dragged through the streets to the scaffold at Smithfield. This was to allow the crowds to inflict the dreadful humiliation of spitting and tipping pots of urine and faeces on the convicted traitor. Wallace had suffered worse, being whipped, beaten and pelted with refuse and rotten food. On the scaffold the naked prisoner was first hanged by his neck from a beam. As he retched, choked and involuntarily defecated, his executioners watched carefully and let the victim crash to the ground moments before he was asphyxiated. Sometimes a bucket of cold water was thrown to revive those who had lost consciousness. At that point, and this would certainly have been done to Robert Bruce, the traitor was emasculated, the cutting off of his testicles symbolic of the end of his treacherous line. The blood-soaked handful was held up for the jeers and cheers of the crowd. More appalling agonies waited for those still conscious when the executioners took a butcher's cleaver to slice open their abdomen from neck to groin so that they could 'draw' out the steaming entrails. Often they were burnt on a brazier and reports exist of men being conscious and able to witness this barbarity. At that point the prisoner was dragged to the block for the merciful release of beheading. And then the body was chopped with the cleavers into quarters and distributed for display. This dreadful ritual was unhesitatingly meted out by Edward I's busy executioners again and again during the Wars of Independence.

But when Comyn whispered, Bruce had friends who overheard. One winter's night in the Tower, when Edward I had drunk a little too much wine, he let slip that he planned to arrest the traitor. Raoul de Monthermer, Earl of Gloucester, had probably already warned Bruce that something was in the air and when he heard the old king mutter in his cups that the Scot was to be detained the following day, he sent what sounds like an unwritten but well understood message. Gloucester's keeper of the wardrobe gave Bruce twelve pennies and a pair of spurs. The latter spoke of haste and the former had Edward I's head on them. Wasting no time, Bruce sent the pennies back to Gloucester and with a squire quietly saddled horses and rode like the wind for Scotland. There was no going back now.

After five days' hard riding, no doubt constantly looking

over his shoulder for pursuers, Bruce reached his family castle at Lochmaben in Dumfriesshire. As he related what had happened in London, it seemed that fate was conspiring. When Robert was later told that John Comyn was at Dumfries, he sent word seeking a meeting. It was set for 10 February, 1306. Reports of what happened and why it happened do not agree.

In the *Scotichronicon*, Walter Bower recounts a remarkable series of coincidences. On the same day as Bruce was arriving at Lochmaben, he met a solitary man walking along the track. It just so happened that he was carrying letters from John Comyn to Edward I detailing Bruce's treachery and making certain the grisly execution that would surely follow. After these had been removed from his person, the poor man was beheaded, allegedly. Bower went on to describe the meeting between Comyn and Bruce at the Greyfriars Kirk in Dumfries as a showdown, with the said letters as exhibit A. Accusations soon descended into violence and 'a fatal blow was dealt in this same church on this slanderer'. There then followed the famous and probably apocryphal return of Sir James de Lindsay to the church to 'mak siccar' and finish off the wounded Comyn.

Less colourful but likely more accurate is the picture painted by other sources, notably the English chronicler, Walter de Guisborough. John Comyn was enormously powerful in Scotland, a real obstacle to Bruce's royal ambitions and either his support or his removal was necessary. What happened at the Greyfriars in February 1306 may have been unpremeditated, a fatal flare-up, but the neutralising of the Comyn leadership was essential. And the murder propelled Robert Bruce at breakneck speed down the road to destiny.

In only six weeks between the sacrilege in Dumfries and his

coronation at Scone, Bruce and his supporters seized several castles in the south-west and secured the alliance with Clan Donald and their chief, Aonghas Og. Far from condemning the brutal murder done in front of the high altar at Greyfriars, Robert Wishart, Bishop of Glasgow, threw all of his considerable support and resources behind Bruce. And in the sort of moment that can colour history vividly, the old bishop brought out of his treasury two items that he had kept hidden, waiting upon events. Edward I had not only removed the Stone of Destiny but had also taken much of Scotland's royal regalia. But Wishart showed Bruce a set of vestments fit for a king to wear at his coronation and a silken royal banner blazoned with the lion and scarlet lilies. A flag that would fly for Scotland.

John Balliol still lived. And despite his humiliation at Montrose, he was still seen by many magnates as the rightful king of Scotland. More, he had in the shape of his son, Edward, a full-grown heir who could establish a stable dynasty. In the eyes of the law and of natural justice, Bruce was unquestionably a usurper and as he, Wishart and his supporters rode to Scone, to the ancient crowning place of Scottish kings since the days of Kenneth MacAlpin, what they needed above all was legitimacy.

In 2007 magnetic resonance imaging technology began to produce startling results as it traced the outline of a large, lost building, a place central to the unfolding of Scotland's history. In the grounds of Scone Palace, the seat of the earls of Mansfield, computer screens flickered as the foundations of a church more than 100 metres in length showed up. Archaeologists had found the lost abbey, the great medieval church where Robert Bruce was inaugurated in 1306. No stone had been left standing upon another after a mob of fervent reformers from Dundee had destroyed Scone Abbey in 1559. But twenty-first-century technology had at last revealed the place where Robert Wishart, Bishop of Glasgow, had robed the new king in his splendid vestments and where the standard of the royal lion of Scotland and the scarlet lilies had been unfurled.

Hard by the site of the abbey stands an eminence of greater antiquity and perhaps even greater significance. The Moot Hill is an artificial mound where the early Celtic kings of Scotland underwent the rituals of coronation. The close propinquity of these two remarkable structures in fact symbolises a cultural divide, which would eventually become a clash in medieval Scotland, one that Robert Bruce knew he had to resolve.

In the great abbey, the Christian elements of coronation, many of these borrowed from Frankish practice, were enacted. As processions with crosses at their head glided up the nave to take their places near the high altar, bishops made ready to anoint the new king and give into his hands the familiar symbols of his office. As they still are, a ring, a sword and a sceptre were bestowed on the monarch. A series of solemn oaths were sworn in God's name and a crown placed on the king's head. After the coronation of Charlemagne as Holy Roman Emperor on Christmas Day, 800, when the Pope appeared to solemnise a political reality, the Church had attempted to fashion these ceremonies as a sacred compact between God and sovereigns. In 1306, Robert Bruce was almost certainly dressed in the vestments from Glasgow Cathedral by Bishop Wishart and the flag with the lion and scarlet lilies was no doubt brought into the church and planted near the high altar, and the chair that acted as a throne. In a reminder of how homemade the ceremony was, a chronicler noted that there was in fact no crown. Edward I had removed the Scottish crown jewels and a circlet of gold had to be quickly forged so that Wishart could set it on Bruce's bare head.

The organisers knew that the coronation needed to be well attended and it appears that the Scottish clergy came in force to Scone. The Bishop of Glasgow was joined by William Lamberton of St Andrews, the man who had made a pact of mutual support with Bruce at the siege of Stirling in 1302. Standing beside the two senior bishops at the high altar were also Bishop David Murray of Moray, the bishops of Dunkeld and Brechin, their host, Abbot Henry of Scone and probably the Abbot of Inchcolm. Temporal power entered the church with the Earls of Mar, Menteith, Atholl and Lennox, as well as many of King Robert's own family and supporters. It seems that a large contingent of men of lesser rank, those who might be termed lairds, also rode to Scone to bear witness. Men like Thomas Hay of Borthwick in Midlothian, Alexander Seton and Neil Campbell of Lochawe in Argyll. Their presence in numbers reinforced the notion of election as well as coronation, the sense that Bruce had been chosen by the community of the realm. And that John Balliol had been rejected as a failed king.

An important absentee was Duncan, Earl of Fife. Since earliest times, his predecessors had held the right of crowning, the placing of the crown on the new king's head. But Duncan had been warded by Edward I. This presented Wishart and the others with a problem. His absence might be critical. Legitimacy and the imperative to do all in accordance with tradition in what was, in the eyes of the law, the coronation of a usurper, meant that the inability of the Earl of Fife to crown the king could have invalidated everything. Perhaps at the insistence of Wishart or Lamberton, urgent messages were sent to Isabel, Countess of Buchan. She was Earl

Duncan's aunt and a scion of the house of Fife. Isabel could crown Bruce as a representative and tradition could be served. But there were difficulties. Her husband, John Comyn, Earl of Buchan, was a supporter of Edward I and in March 1306 was at his manor in Leicestershire. And how would a mere woman make her way to Scone? She appears to have thought of that and it is said that she had kept her husband's warhorses with her and that they allowed her to come to the abbey in appropriate style, like a relative of a great magnate, a person of substance. But messages did not reach the countess quickly enough. It seems that Bruce was crowned on 23 March 1306 – without Isabel of Buchan. Two days later, she arrived at Scone and so vital was her presence, the ceremony was repeated. The countess would later endure terrible suffering for her defiance of her husband and Edward I.

Bruce's reign dates formally from 25 March 1306, the Feast of the Annunciation. Isabel of Buchan had crowned a king and also made a queen. But Elizabeth Bruce was less than impressed. She is said to have taken a cold-eyed view of the political and military realities. When Bruce sounded a note of triumph: 'Rejoice now, my wife, because you have been made a queen and I a king', Walter of Guisborough noted her sober rejoinder: 'I am afraid my lord that we have been made king and queen, as boys are made in summer games.' Or King and Queen of the May, as others had it.

In the eyes of many of his subjects, especially his key allies from the Atlantic seaboard and the south-west, the ceremonies and the anthems in Scone Abbey did not mean that Bruce had been fully inaugurated as their king. It is very likely that another sort of ceremony took place, that the anointing and oath-swearing in the church were followed by ancient rituals enacted on Moot

Hill. Wishart, Lamberton and the other advisors will have been anxious to follow all traditions closely, even those they did not necessarily approve of. A record of Alexander III's coronation survives in the *Scotichronicon*:

> In accordance with the custom which had grown up in the kingdom from antiquity right up to that time, after the solemn ceremony of the king's coronation, the bishops with the earls brought the king to the cross which stands in the cemetery on the east side of the church [the site of Moot Hill]. With due reverence they installed him there on the royal seat [the Stone of Destiny] which had been bedecked with silk cloths embroidered with gold. So when the king was solemnly seated on this royal seat of stone, with his crown on his head and his sceptre in his hand, and clothed in royal purple, and at his feet the earls and other nobles were setting down their stools to listen to a sermon, there suddenly appeared a venerable, grey-haired figure, an elderly Scot. Though a wild Highlander, he was honourably attired after his own fashion, clad in a scarlet robe. Bending his knee in a scrupulously correct manner, he greeted the king in his mother tongue, saying courteously: 'God bless the King of Albany, Alexander macAlexander, macWilliam, macHenry, macDavid . . .'
>
> Then this same Scot read right through the aforesaid genealogy, linking up each person with the next, until he came to the first Scot, that is Hiber the Scot. This Iber was the son of Gaythelos, the son of Neolus

> formerly King of the Athenians by Scota, daughter of the King of Egypt, the pharoah Chencres.

The ethnonyms and the journey back through the mists of myth-history were important in the ancient Gaelic ritual of the *sloin-neadh*, the naming of the names of memory. Not only did their recital demonstrate the unbroken right of a new king to rule, the names also emerged from the hallowed past to stand beside him as he took his place on the Stone of Destiny. The ghosts of an immense history conferred both solemnity and legitimacy and in 1306, it is certain that an *ollamh righ*, the king's bard, will have recited Bruce's genealogy and his royal descent from Earl Henry, just as had been done for Alexander III. And the Gaelic-speaking Earl of Carrick will have understood every word.

The pre-Christian rituals of Moot Hill were not always so welcome. In 1124 David I was appalled. According to his friend and chronicler, Aelred of Rievaulx, the anglicised, Normanised young king 'so abhorred those acts of homage which are offered by the Scottish nation in the manner of their fathers upon the recent promotion of their kings, that he was with difficulty compelled by the bishops to receive them'. On the hill, it is likely that kings were wedded to their nation and their people in a version of a fertility rite. And what probably horrified the urbane David was the sense of symbolism. If, like a stallion or a bull, a king was entire, healthy and sexually vigorous, then these were all attributes that would somehow be reflected in a flourishing Scotland. Recent dynastic politics will also have added to his unease. When David's uncle, King Donald III Ban, seized the kingship on the death of his brother, he rejected the newfangled fashion of primogeniture and reverted to the Celtic principles of succession and drove out all the Anglo-Normans who had come north. The young David fled with them. Donald Ban's reign was a clear reversion to ancient kingship, what was celebrated on Moot Hill. In 1099, he was deposed by David's elder brother, Edgar, and imprisoned then blinded. And this was done to invalidate his claims to the throne and shrivel traditional support. To rule, a Celtic king had to be whole and healthy, and when Edgar ordered that his uncle's eyes should be put out, he knew he had ended his royal pretensions.

A hefty item of cultural luggage, the Stone of Destiny reinforced the links with a long past. Tradition held that it came from the Irish equivalent of Moot Hill, the sacred Hill of Tara. Brought across the North Channel to the colony of Dalriada by Simon Brecc, it was placed at Scone by Fergus macFerchair. At Tara, the coronation stone was said to roar if a rightful king was ordained. Perhaps on Moot Hill it roared twice in March 1306.

The name of Scone also hints at ancient ceremonial. Gaelic poetry supplied subtitles. The site of coronation was hailed as *Scoine sciath-airde*, or Scone of the High Shields. This looks like a reference to the habit of warriors of raising a king on their shields and a second epithet appears to confirm that as it adds a soundtrack. Bards also sang of *Scoine sciath-bhinne*, Scone of the Singing Shields, probably a reference to the formula of acclamation itself. Perhaps the fastidious, forward-looking David I, French-speaking and educated at the court of Henry I, found it all a little primitive, backward-looking. It is unlikely that Robert Bruce shared his diffidence – he could not afford to.

Despite the naming of the names and the dual ceremonies, the new reign began badly. Outraged at Bruce's treachery and his demand to be recognised as king, Edward I appointed Aymer de

Valence as his de facto governor of Scotland. A highly capable soldier, he was given direct orders to raise the dragon banner, the terrifying sign that none would be spared as the English army blazed its way through Scotland. The houses and farms of Bruce's supporters were burned and many killed. Bishops Wishart and Lamberton were quickly captured and sent south to the royal dungeons in chains, only their episcopal rank saving them from the grisly fate of traitors. By June 1306, de Valence had taken the town of Perth and the new king felt compelled to act. Bruce was about to make a series of serious blunders and learn some sharp lessons.

At the head of a substantial army, flushed with the confidence of his coronation, the new king rode up to the walls of Perth and challenged Aymer de Valence to come out and fight on open ground. When the English governor refused, Bruce led his men to make camp at Methven, a short distance west of Perth. There the Scots bivouacked, foraged for food and failed to set pickets. In the early hours of 19 June 1306, de Valence mounted a surprise attack and after some initial resistance, scattered the Scots. With only a few hundred survivors, Bruce fled into the mountains and glens of the west. And the savagery promised by the dragon banner saw sixteen of Bruce's supporters executed, two of them suffering the terrible death of traitors.

After another setback near Tyndrum, where his small force was defeated by John MacDougall of Argyll, Bruce sent Queen Elizabeth and their daughter, Marjorie, north to Kildrummy Castle in Aberdeenshire. The Earl of Atholl, Neil Bruce, Alexander Lindsay and Robert Boyd rode with the party as escorts. All were eventually captured and taken south to Berwick, where many of the men were hanged, drawn and quartered. For her part in the coronation, for adding the appearance of legitimacy, the Countess of Buchan was put into a cage made from iron and wood which was suspended over the walls of Berwick Castle where, according to Walter of Guisborough, 'she could be seen and recognised by those passing by. And she remained many days, thus enclosed and on a strict regimen'. Bruce's sister, Mary, suffered the same dreadful fate at Roxburgh Castle and far from 'many days', both women lived in these cages through four winters and countless storms of wind and rain. Their only respite was the use of a toilet inside the castles' walls. Shivering, often soaked to the skin and always ridiculed, caged like animals, it is astonishing that these tough women survived. Consistently cruel, Edward I had demanded that a similar cage be made for the 12-year-old Marjorie Bruce and be hung over the battlements of the Tower of London, but he was later persuaded to relent. Instead the little girl was immured in a nunnery in Yorkshire for eight years.

King Robert had every reason to despair. It seems that after meeting his one steadfast ally, Aonghas Og MacDonald, he wintered on the tiny island of Rathlin, off the coast of Ulster. It was imperative he avoid capture on the mainland. It may have been there that the parable of the spider was spun. Watching the insect make repeated attempts to attach its web to the walls of a cave, Bruce took heart, especially when it finally succeeded. Almost certainly an invention or adaptation of another tale by Walter Scott, the message of the parable was apt. Bruce had to persist. And he did.

Two Christian women quickly came to his aid. Here is the relevant passage from the *Scotichronicon*:

> When the king had endured these adversities alone for about a year, finally at the inspiration of God, aided

> by the assistance and power of a certain woman of noble rank, Christiana of the Isles, who was well-disposed to him, after many and various roundabout journeys and innumerable toils, pains and afflictions, he returned to his earldom of Carrick.

But then Bruce blundered again when he sent his brothers, Thomas and Alexander, to Galloway. Both were captured and suffered the agonies of the scaffold as they too were hanged, drawn and quartered. Bruce may have been at his lowest ebb at that moment. All of the castles of his earldom were in enemy hands and he and his dwindling band of men were fugitives in the hills. And then fate, perhaps even sentiment, took a hand. Christian of Carrick was said to have been Bruce's lover and she brought him 40 men. It was a beginning. With these reinforcements, Christian also brought news and she told King Robert what had happened to his womenfolk and the miserable humiliations of Isabella of Buchan and his sister, Mary.

Despite these ill tidings, Bruce's fortunes began quickly to improve. Realising that he would never succeed by opposing the superior English forces in open field, he resolved to go against all his chivalric instincts and fight a guerrilla war. Through stealth, ambush, the choice of ground and speed of movement, Bruce would patiently build his strength. His new strategy was best expressed in poetic form, what became known as Good King Robert's Testament:

> On foot should be all Scottish war,
> Let hill and marsh their foes debar,
> And woods as walls prove such an arm,

> That enemies do them no harm,
> In hidden spots keep every store,
> And burn the plainlands them before,
> So, when they find the land lie waste,
> Needs must they pass away in haste,
> Harried by cunning raids at night,
> And threatening sounds from every height,
> Then, as they leave with great array,
> Smite with the sword and chase away.
> This is the counsel and intent,
> Of Good King Robert's Testament.

Three days after his success against Aymer de Valence at Loudoun Hill in May 1307, the Scots king attacked another English force, this one commanded by the Earl of Gloucester, the same Raoul de Monthermer who had warned Bruce of Edward I's intentions in 1302. It was a rout and the English were chased back to the safety of the walls of the town of Ayr. Momentum seemed at last to be swinging towards the Scots and it may be that news of Edward I's ill health was leaking out. Here is a fascinating letter dated 15 May 1307 from a Scots nobleman, probably based somewhere in or around Forfar, who supported the English king:

> I hear that Bruce never had the goodwill of his own followers or of the people generally so much with him as now. It appears that God is with him, for he has destroyed King Edward's power both amongst English and Scots. The people believe that Bruce will carry all before him, exhorted by 'false preachers' from Bruce's army, men who have been previously charged before the

> justices for advocating war and have been released on bail, but are now behaving worse then ever. I fully believe, as I have heard from Reginald Cheyne, Duncan of Frendraught, and Gilbert of Glencarnie, who keep the peace beyond the Mounth [north of Stonehaven] and on this side, that if Bruce can get away in this direction or towards the parts of Ross he will find the people all ready at his will more entirely than ever, unless King Edward can send more troops, for there are many people living loyally in his peace so long as the English are in power. May it please God to prolong King Edward's life, for men say openly that when he is gone the victory will go to Bruce. For these preachers have told the people that they have found a prophecy of Merlin, that after the death of 'le Roy Coveytous' the people of Scotland and the Welsh shall band together and have full lordship and live in peace together to the end of the world.

Once again prophecy and widespread belief in it seemed powerful, and when news came north in July 1307 that Edward I, the Hammer of the Scots, had died at Burgh by Sands, there was a seismic political shift, what the perceptive letter-writer had predicted. The compiler of the *Lanercost Chronicle* agreed: 'Despite the fearful revenge inflicted upon the Scots who adhered to Bruce, the number of those willing to strengthen him in his kingship increased daily.' Described as 'a great and terrible king', Edward's uncompromising ruthlessness and the fear his certain retribution struck into the hearts of waverers was suddenly removed from political calculation. His son, now proclaimed Edward II, proved to be easily diverted and his appetites would soon cause dissent amongst the great English magnates. Bruce must have been much buoyed by the news from the Solway coast.

The death of the great and terrible king also gave Robert Bruce precious time to establish himself and deal with his enemies in Scotland. Preoccupied with domestic difficulties, Edward II did not lead an army north for three years. In addition, he further buttressed the Bruce cause by replacing Aymer de Valence with the Earl of Richmond as governor of Scotland. He was much less effective and experienced. This twin respite allowed the new king to begin the slow business of winning his kingdom.

In the latter half of 1307 Bruce broke out of his Galloway heartland and moved north to link with Aonghas Og and his fleet of birlinns. Their oarsmen acted as marines and could strike quickly and unexpectedly at coastal targets. In the twelfth century the shipwrights of the Macdonald Lords of the Isles had developed the birlinns, the *nybhaig*, or little ships. With a shallow draught and a hinged rudder fixed to the stern instead of a steer-board over one side, these galleys were extremely manoeuvrable, better able to sail amongst the rocky reefs of the Hebridean coasts and make landfall where the larger longships could not.

When the MacDougalls were forced to seek a truce, Bruce turned his gaze further north, to the Moray coastlands and the power-base of the Comyns, his greatest Scottish enemies. Having ridden up the Great Glen, capturing castles at Inverlochy, Urquhart and Inverness, the king joined forces with Bishop David of Moray, who had attended the coronation at Scone but avoided capture. As great magnates, bishops could muster substantial bodies of soldiers, but the combined forces first moved against the Earl of Ross, their threats extracting a useful truce. Now they could deal with the Comyns.

After a bout of illness (Bruce had been driving himself relentlessly for a year and a half) and a retreat, battle was eventually joined at Inverurie in the centre of the great estates of the Comyns. On 23 May 1308, the Earl of Buchan was defeated. Bruce ordered Edward, by now his only surviving brother, to begin what became known at the herschip of Buchan, the harrying of the wide lands of the Comyns in the north-east. Deliberately brutal, the killings and burnings were set as an example and more lords were persuaded that Bruce would prevail as the defeated earl fled to England.

By 1309 the English occupation of Scotland was much reduced. After the terror campaign in Buchan, Bruce and his captains held most of Scotland north of the Forth and they were also in control of the south-west. Garrisons loyal to Edward II held Stirling, Edinburgh, Roxburgh and Berwick castles and, with them, the hinterlands of the Lothians and the Borders. Bruce knew that these were perhaps the most valuable regions of his kingdom, and that much unfinished military business waited, but he also realised that he needed to begin to behave like Robert I, King of Scotland. He needed to hold a parliament.

On 16 and 17 March 1309 what came to be called the Community of the Realm assembled at St Andrews. With its vast medieval cathedral, the greatest church in all Scotland, dominating the headland that juts into the North Sea, with its precious relics of an apostle, a man who knew Christ, and its streets laid out as ceremonial ways to and from the west door of the church, the town could fairly claim to be the spiritual capital of the nation. As magnates, prelates and lesser lairds rode east along the pilgrims' ways, breasting the rise at Strathkinness or rounding the shore road at Guardbridge, the spires of the cathedral announced the sorts of solemn associations with a venerable Christian past that the supporters of the new king needed.

Records of the proceedings of the parliament (almost certainly held in the cathedral) are sparse, but from another quarter came a great boost to the sense of Bruce's wider legitimacy. King Philip IV of France had written requesting Scottish help in a crusade and he talked of his 'special love' of King Robert. Just as it is now, international recognition of new regimes was important and Philip IV had even described Bruce as 'King of Scots' in a letter to Edward II. Very sensibly the Scots pointed out to the French king that their country had suffered repeatedly at the hands of invading English armies and that consequently there was no possibility of sending soldiers on crusade, at least not in the near future. But, wrote Bruce's clerks, once all of the present difficulties with Edward of England had been resolved, the king himself would lead a Scots contingent to help retrieve the Holy Land from the unbelievers.

This round of diplomacy was helpful but the more pressing business was the need to buttress Bruce's position inside Scotland. His coronation three years before had been the herald of great difficulties and in 1309 Isabella of Buchan and Mary Bruce still shivered in cages slung over the battlements of Berwick and Roxburgh castles. The kingdom was far from secured. What Bruce and his advisors needed was positive show, an acknowledgement that he was much more powerful than he had been at Scone from a gathering of prelates and magnates who could fairly claim to represent the Community of the Realm.

This idea had developed in the years following the death of Alexander III, the kingdom without a king and the era of the Guardians of the Realm. And it grew powerful. The Community's support for Bruce suggested a shadowy sense of election that was to become more manifest in the Declaration of Arbroath of 1320. But for now, a less expansive but nevertheless dramatic statement was made by the St Andrews parliament. Describing themselves as 'the bishops, abbots, priors and others of the clergy duly constituted in the realm of Scotland', they issued what amounted to a communiqué. It not only asserted Scotland's right to independence but also supported Bruce's claim to the throne as having always been superior to Balliol's. It was the birth of the idea that King John had been little better than a sub-king, a puppet of the Plantagenet kings of England.

There were notable absentees in St Andrews Cathedral. In addition to the Comyns, the Macdougalls and those who remained loyal to the Balliols, the earls of Angus, Atholl and Dunbar, did not attend. The Community of the Realm could by no means be called complete. And nor was Robert Bruce's control of Scotland. The Lothians and the Borders were still held by the king's enemies and only a few months after the parliament had been adjourned, Edward II began to mass invasion forces.

Sir Robert Clifford led one army up the western approaches to occupy Carlisle and establish headquarters in the old Roman city's squat and dour castle. But Bruce refused to be drawn into pitched battle, and in any case it was late in the year. Clifford agreed a winter truce, a tactic well understood by the Lanercost chronicler: 'the English do not willingly enter Scotland to wage war before summer chiefly because earlier in the year they find no food for their horses'. The Earl of Hereford had led a second force up the eastern roads to Berwick and while it is unclear whether or not the Carlisle truce applied to both, it is likely that the English commanders sent the bulk of their soldiers home.

Almost a year later, on 8 September 1310, Edward II's clerks issued a new summons to join the royal host. Even though only three earls, Cornwall (that is, Piers Gaveston), Gloucester and Surrey came in person, the army was large. And increasingly hungry. Refusing battle, Bruce scorched the earth in front of the English advance and when Edward II moved his forces from Berwick to Biggar, his quartermasters found that virtually no supplies could be bought or commandeered in Berwickshire, Roxburghshire or Peeblesshire. In fact the Borders was suffering localised famine as a result of Bruce's ruthless actions. Added to which, James Douglas' guerrilla forces used the cover of the Ettrick Forest and the wild hill country of the Southern Uplands as bases for harrying the English advance. Only seven weeks after his summons to muster, the English king was forced to march back to Berwick, having accomplished nothing. The author of *The Life of Edward II* was perilously close to congratulating Bruce, the man his readers ridiculed as King Hob. But his tactics in 1310 were far from ridiculous:

> For Robert Bruce, knowing himself unequal to the strength of the King of England in strength or fortune, decided that it would be better to resist our king by secret warfare rather than dispute his right in open battle. Indeed, I might be tempted to sound the praises of Sir Robert did not the guilt of homicide and the dark stain of treachery bid me keep silent.

Although Edward II had used Berwick as a headquarters from which he could tighten his grip on the Lothians and the Borders by installing seasoned commanders and garrisons in the likes of

Roxburgh and Edinburgh castles, there was a sense that history was shifting, that sentiment and the initiative were moving towards Bruce. Lanercost Priory near Carlisle had accommodated Edward I and his son's commanders but its chronicler seems almost sympathetic to those who lived in the borderlands and the Lothians, in the path of invading armies and Bruce's raids into England.

> In all this fighting the Scots were so divided that often a father was with the Scots and his son with the English, or one brother was with the Scots and another with the English, or even one individual was first on one side and then on the other. But all or most of the Scots who were with the English were with them insincerely or to save their lands in England; for their hearts if not their bodies were always with their own people.

More diplomacy underpinned Bruce's growing international stature. In 1266 Alexander III had concluded the Treaty of Perth with the King of Norway and its terms conceded the formalisation (after the Battle of Largs) of the passing of the Hebrides into the realm of Scotland. Norway was nominally compensated by a perpetual annuity of 100 merks. On October 1312 envoys despatched by Haakon V arrived in Perth to renew the treaty with the Scots king, thereby recognising the right and title of Robert Bruce. Along with Philip IV of France's support in 1309, this exchange of seals and signatures added more weight to the new king's authority. And as an uneasy peace descended over much of Scotland, trade with northern Europe out of the North Sea ports began tentatively to resume.

As the Scots moved on with the patient business of reconquest, the taking of castles and strongholds piecemeal, Bruce achieved an unlikely but spectacular coup. The Isle of Man had recently been in English hands, but only a century before it had formed part of the sea-kingdom of the Lordship of the Isles. The great Somerled had been crowned King of Man. In May 1313, with a large fleet (which must have included the birlinns of Aonghas Og Macdonald) Robert Bruce disembarked an expedition at Ramsey and, moving quickly south to Castletown, laid siege to Rushen Castle. In three weeks it fell, and while it is unclear as to whether or not Bruce laid claim to the old kingship, his daring and military reach were impressive. But his absence from Scotland had important consequences.

While King Robert rode down the coast road to Douglas and Castletown, his brother Edward was besieging Stirling Castle. And when he made his fateful offer of a year's truce to Sir Philip Moubray, the governor of the garrison, it seems that messages seeking advice or consultation were not sent to Man. Bruce's anger at his brother's rashness was recorded by John Barbour:

> When Sir Edward, as I told you, had given so extreme a day for the surrender or rescue of Stirling, he went very soon to the king and told what negotiations he had had and what day he had given them. The king when he heard the day said: 'That was unwisely done, perfay, I never yet heard of where so long a warning was given to so mighty a king as the King of England is. Because he now has in his hands England, Ireland, and Wales too, yes, and Aquitaine, with all those who

> live under his lordship, and still a part of Scotland. He is so well provided with treasure, that he can have abundance of mercenaries. [But] we are few against so many. God may assign our destinies right well, but we are placed to lose or win them speedily.'

Once his anger with his brother had cooled, Bruce began to set in train a series of events that would lead to the great muster at the Tor Wood in May 1314.

A village of the same name still appears on modern maps and a remnant of woodland is marked as the Tor Wood in the triangle of farmland bounded by three motorways, the M9, the M80 and the M876. But in the early fourteenth century the forested area was much more extensive, stretching from the Carron Water in the south to the Bannock Burn in the north. East lay the Forth and the treacherous marshlands of its foreshore and to the west rose the hills of the Bannauc, the ancient barrier between the old territory of Scotia and Scotland south of the line of the Antonine Wall. The name came from the Gaelic word *torr* for a mound or eminence, or by extension, a heap of stones. This may well have been a reference to the broch at Tappoch. Perched on a mound 380 feet above sea level, its substantial remains are still surrounded by the remnant of the Tor Wood and they suggest a building that would have dominated the landscape. Not only does the broch afford excellent views in all directions, it rises only 200 yards west of the Roman road.

The Tor Wood was an excellent focus for a muster. Accessible easily from north and south, only two to three miles from Stirling and astride the route Edward's army would have to take, it saw contingents of soldiers begin to arrive from the middle of

May onwards. Bruce no doubt encouraged early arrival, even with its attendant logistical problems of supply, for his men and their captains had work to do. If they were to stand firm in their formations of spearmen, or learn to advance and reform, the Scots infantry would have to learn to move as coherent units.

Schiltron or sometimes schiltrom was the name given to the bristling ranks of spearmen who were at the heart of the armies of William Wallace and Robert Bruce. First mentioned in the historical record in 1297 at the Battle of Falkirk, the word originally meant something like a shield-wall, or at any rate a very tight infantry formation. The schiltrons commanded by Wallace were circular and essentially static, designed to resist and wear down charging knights. What undid the Scottish schiltrons in 1297 was archery, the relentless volleys thinning the ranks followed by a series of devastating cavalry charges.

At the Tor Wood and when the army marched the short distance to the New Park, it is likely that Bruce and his captains took much time and trouble to train their men to move precisely in formation. To make the schiltron dynamic, to convert it from a defensive to an attacking unit, it was vital that any movement was carefully coordinated. Scraps of evidence and analogy hint at how this might have been achieved.

A clear and effective command structure was necessary and in the *Scotichronicon*, Walter Bower described William Wallace's ruthless imposition of discipline amongst his spearmen:

> For he encouraged his comrades in arms towards the achievement of whatever plan he had in hand always to approach battle for the liberty of their homeland with one mind. And as regards the whole multitude

> of his followers he decreed on pain of death that once the lesser men among the middling people (or in practice those who were less robust) had been assembled before him, one man was always to be chosen out of five from all the groups of five to be over the other four and called a quaternion; his commands were to be obeyed by them in all matters, and whoever did not obey was to be killed. In a similar manner also moving on up to the men who were more robust and effective there was always to be tenth man [called a decurion] over each nine, and a twentieth over each nineteen, and so on moving up to each thousand [called a chiliarch] and beyond to the top. At length, he himself as preeminent over everyone else and was regarded as commander or general, whom all were bound to obey to the death. With everyone harmoniously approving this law (or substitute for the law), they chose him as their captain, and promised to keep the said statute until the succession of a legitimate king.

It is likely that as a legitimate king and with the agreement of his commanders, Bruce imitated this structure, which may in turn have been copied by Wallace from an English example. Schiltrons could not move quickly for a tight formation needed to be maintained at all times. And in the din and chaos of battle, it is almost certain that trumpets or bugles were used to signal orders from the likes of Randolph or Douglas and drums to beat out an even marching time. If any gaps opened because of uneven pace, they could be fatal. It seems more than likely that schiltrons drilled together in the long summer days at the Tor Wood and at the New

Park. Every one of the men chosen to fight knew that good discipline might make the difference between life and death.

In 1318 King Robert's administration issued an arming act, the earliest ever promulgated in Scotland, and it revealed something of how spearmen were dressed and armed as they drilled four years before. In order to recruit as many men as possible, the qualification for army service was set low at a value of £10 in goods, not land. This was probably so that they could include burgesses. Each man needed a padded jacket, a bassinet or metal helmet, gloves of plate, a mail coat if possible, a sword or dirk and a spear.

In modern illustrations of medieval battles spearmen are often shown wielding perfectly straight, perfectly uniform and perfectly turned spear-shafts, each with an identical iron point riveted to the business end. These illustrations cannot be accurate. Machine-sawn and turned timber did not appear until the eighteenth century and the reality at the Tor Wood must have been a great deal more homemade. Ten- or twelve-foot shafts are likely to have been cut from coppiced hardwood. There is a tradition that ash was preferred. Whatever was cut needed to be seasoned, and since coppiced and other saplings grew thicker at the base than at the tip, great care and knowledge will have been needed in selection. The butt-end of a spear-shaft could not be thicker than the span of a man's hand. And unseasoned or green wood would have been too whippy and elastic, likely to waggle at the tip and be difficult to direct. No doubt shafts were smoothed by abrasives but a few knobbly imperfections might have made a grip more secure. In any event, the length of the spears in schiltrons also made for slow and deliberate movement.

Much better documented were the tactics and training of

the well-drilled pike squares of the fifteenth-century Swiss Confederacy, and their set moves may have been developments of what was rehearsed at the Tor Wood. Usually organised into units of 100 men, the front rank prepared for the charge of armoured knights by kneeling and butting their pikes into the ground while the second rank pointed theirs over their heads or even rested them on their comrades' shoulders. So nimble were the Swiss pikemen that they could change direction quickly and thereby make it very difficult for cavalry to outflank them. Again, archers and crossbowmen were a threat, but so strong and confident were the Swiss that they could charge with pikes levelled. On Europe's battlefields, these formations were greatly feared.

Once Bruce had led his men from the Tor Wood to the New Park, he and his commanders will have considered the ground, where it would be most advantageous to fight the far more numerous and better equipped army of Edward II, an army that was moving closer to Stirling as the days lengthened and the midsummer solstice approached.

4
The March Against Time

The Feast of St Botolph, the 17th day of June 1314.

Sir Aymer de Valence knew the ground. As Edward I's military commander in Scotland he had both defeated Robert Bruce at Methven in 1306 and been defeated by him a year later at Loudoun Hill. Communications will have been vital to the Earl of Pembroke as he governed in the king's name, making sure castle garrisons were well provisioned, taxes collected, rebellious Scots checked and contained. By the time Edward II led his vast army splashing across the Tweed below Wark Castle, de Valence had ridden ahead with a substantial vanguard. On his last, fruitless expedition to Scotland, the king and his forces had been harried by the hit-and-run tactics of the light cavalry of James Douglas, skirmishers on tough and shaggy little ponies who seemed to come charging out of nowhere. And as the royal host clambered up the Scottish bank of the Tweed on Monday, 17 June 1314, Pembroke was charged with sweeping the countryside in front of the English advance. If Edward II were to relieve Stirling Castle by midsummer, Monday, 24 June, he had only a week to cover the 80 miles from Wark. He could not afford to be delayed or diverted by Douglas' horsemen or any other tactic devised by the Scots king who was preparing, waiting for him at the Tor Wood. Edward knew he was marching against time.

Not that the undulating fields of the Berwickshire countryside offered much cover for surprise attacks, even on stragglers as the English army inevitably began to string out in a long line. De Valence knew that because he had probably ridden its roads and tracks several times before on his way from Roxburgh Castle to Berwick. In 1290, Edward I concluded the Treaty of Birgham, a small village only a mile west of Wark but on the Scottish side of the Tweed, and one of the signatories had been William de Valence, Aymer's father and Earl of Pembroke before him. At that time the boy was a squire probably serving a knight in the service of the earl and may well have been in his retinue at Birgham. At the Treaty Field commissioners agreed that Margaret, the little Maid of Norway, would become betrothed to Edward of Caernarvon and thereby bring Scotland and England together in an early version of the union of the crowns. But the Maid died and the match was never completed.

In the text of the treaty Birgham is spelled Briggeham and local archaeologists believe that in the Middle Ages there was almost certainly a reason for the older place-name. Below the village there seems to have been a bridge across the Tweed to the English side. If it was possible to get the ox-drawn carts of vital, and heavy, supplies across the river without risking broken axles or wheels on the rocky bed of the ford below the castle, then that may have greatly reinforced the choice of Wark as a place of muster for the armies of Edward I and his son. And bridges tend to form part of a transport network. If wheeled carts could be pulled across, then it likely that at either end of the Birgham bridge there was a road – and not a track – that allowed them to continue their journey.

Edward's army moved only as fast as its slowest elements would allow, and its route was also dictated by the need for a road that could accommodate the plodding ox-carts. De Valence and the vanguard of mounted knights could trot ahead to scout and scour the country for any supplies, but the infantry, the archers, the king and his retinue needed to march at the pace of the oxen in order to protect their valuable loads. If a cart carrying horsehoes had been captured by marauders or lost in a ford, then the destriers up ahead would not prance for long. Edward II's fundamental logistical difficulty was that once his army entered Scotland, he had no reliable bases where supplies could have been stockpiled ahead of his advance and protected. He needed to bring virtually everything with his army.

Flicking and cracking their long whips in the air over the backs of their ox-teams, the carters knew that once across the Tweed, whether by Birgham bridge or the fords at Wark, they needed to find a well-surfaced road whose ruts might be well worn but at least dry and hard in the summer. Fortunately just such a road ran along the north bank of the Tweed.

In the cartulary of Kelso Abbey many documents refer to Roxburgh, the busy inland market for the wool trade. When merchants bought the bulky woolpacks from farmers or their agents who had brought the spring clip to the broad thoroughfare appropriately known as Market Street, they needed to move their purchases downriver to Berwick. Some may have used rafts on the Tweed but others certainly transported them to the port by cart. Having a direct interest in this lucrative trade, the scribes at Kelso recorded the existence of a *via regis*, a royal road between Roxburgh and Berwick. Its route is now lost except for one tantalising reference to 'the abbot's carts' passing the church at Simprim in Berwickshire. Now a ruin and only a hamlet, Simprim lies about three miles north-east of Wark but the line of the *via regis* must have run south-west towards Roxburgh, probably passing close to Birgham and its bridge. It is very likely that once Edward II's lumbering, cumbersome carts and his vast host crossed the Tweed into Scotland, they hurried west on the royal road. Time was short.

Medieval and ancient sources rarely comment on the climate unless it was extreme, and it may be assumed that June 1314 was fine, or at least not wet. As the English army inevitably strung out in a long line on the 15-mile march from Wark to join the Roman road at Dere Street, the biographer of Edward II was moved to write of a: 'Very fine and large army [and all] who were present agreed that never in our time has such an army gone forth from England [with] enough wagons to have stretched for twenty miles if they had lined up end to end.' If that is not an exaggeration, the mounted vanguard must have arrived at the line of the Roman road while the last of the carts were still crossing the Tweed. Moving such a large body of men, animals and supplies across a medieval landscape was a complex and haphazard logistical exercise, even in good summer conditions.

So that stragglers could not be picked off by Scots skirmishers, detachments of soldiers, horsemen and archers will have been placed at regular intervals in the 20-mile line, which in reality must have been shorter. Otherwise it would have been unmanageable over what was a forced march. Whatever its precise length, the English column will have made an awesome sight, the glinting armour, mail and the silk surcoats of the knights and sergeants visible from many viewpoints. And the scale was also head-shaking, endless, as more and more soldiers, riders and carts breasted each rise on the royal road. Those farmers who had prudently removed their families, animals and possessions out of the path of this plodding Leviathan (even though their lords might have been loyal to King Edward, may indeed have been riding with him, no sensible person would risk being within the reach of thousands of soldiers) will have looked south from the low foothills of the Lammermuirs and watched a vast army hurrying slowly to Stirling and midsummer.

The likely halt after the first and gruelling day's march will have been Earlston, the village of Thomas the Rhymer and the castle of the Earl of Dunbar. This noble family remained in the English camp in 1314 and it may be that the king lodged the night in the same castle where Thomas had prophesied the sequence of events that had brought him and his army north. Earlston made sense as a halt because it lay very close to Dere Street, where the Roman engineers had struck up Lauderdale, over the Lammermuirs and down to Edinburgh, the midland valley and Stirling.

In the first century AD, Agricola, the governor of Britannia, had led the legions into what is now Scotland on a mission of conquest, to bring the 'whole island' into the empire. Part of his army had advanced up Dere Street (named later for the Celtic kingdom of Deur in Durham and North Yorkshire, and the road set out from the legionary fortress at York) and a supply depot was established at Trimontium, near Melrose, in the shadow of the three Eildon Hills. The road crossed the Tweed below the fort, close to where the elegant railway viaduct now stands and it then moved north on the west bank of the River Leader. Each mile of Roman road cost thousands of man-hours to make and if bridges or fords were involved, construction took even longer. Therefore the Roman engineers avoided crossing the river until it was absolutely necessary. Edward II's difficulty was to get his straggle of soldiers, cavalry and carts across as soon as possible. Among his and other medieval commanders who moved men through the landscape, Roman roads were seen much as railways were in the ninteenth century. The imperative was to reach one as quickly as possible because the pace of movement would quicken dramatically.

The ancient arteries carried armies for 1,500 years because they had been built for exactly that purpose. The surface was made up as a slightly cambered mound with drainage ditches on either side and the carriageway was wide enough to allow carts or columns travelling in opposite directions to pass each other. The line of Dere Street can be clearly made out as it crosses, arrow-straight, the folds of the Lammermuirs, and the ditches flank a 30-foot wide metalled surface. It was not only a well-used highway in the Middle Ages, the well-defined line of the old road was recognised as a boundary. When the monks at Kelso Abbey wished to be precise about the extent of land granted to them near Oxton in the twelfth century, they noted that its bounds ran:

> from the head of Holdene descending by the Holdene burn to Derestrete and then by Derestrete heading north to Fuleford and, by Samson's divisions, to the Leader ascending in a straight path to the east end of the said town of Hulfkeliston [Oxton], and from the east end of Ulfkiliston taking a straight path by the south street and ascending to Derestrete with the exception of the tofts and crofts of William de Colilaw . . .

Especially at Carolside and Chapel-on-Leader, immediately to the north of Earlston, the valley of the Leader is steep-sided. The geography and sound military sense persuaded the Roman engineers to site the road on the higher ground west of the river. By moving out of the valley, they avoided the mosses and sikes on the banks, as well as seasonal flooding, and they also reduced the risk of ambush as it could only come over the western ridges. No doubt Aymer de Valence and his armoured cavalry swept the countryside in front of Edward II as he led his men deeper into Scotland and north towards Edinburgh on the second day of their march. Throughout the light night before, the strung-out train of wagons no doubt caught up with the vanguard at the head of the column as they creaked and rumbled into Earlston through the summer gloaming.

Even though the army was now moving more easily on the hard surface (where it had survived 1,200 winters) of the Roman road, they were also climbing into the hills. After Oxton, the Lammermuirs rise steeply but the passage may have been safer and better managed. So wide was Dere Street that horsemen could quickly ride up and down the line of march with orders, help and encouragement. Carts broke down but these casualties could be dragged to one side for repair and not block the road for those behind them. A contemporary Scottish source recorded that the king and his retinue had reached the medieval hospital (built as accommodation for pilgrims as well as those who were unwell) at Soutra on the night of 18 June. Its ruins lie next to Dere Street. There Edward dictated a dispatch and his clerks had it sent south to the royal council and the Archbishop of Canterbury. Having marched hard for two days, perhaps for as long as twelve hours each day, and covered at least thirty miles, the English army had kept to their punishing timetable. Below Soutra lay the eastern end of Scotland's midland valley, Edinburgh 16 miles to the north and Fife beyond. The sharp-eyed may have seen the masts of the English fleet anchored in the Firth of Forth. But men were tired, and the king's biographer, perhaps with the benefit of hindsight, noted that:

> He hastened by day to the appointed place, not as if he were leading an army to battle but as if he was on a pilgrimage to St James of Compostella. Brief were the halts for sleep, briefer still for food, hence horses, horsemen and infantry were worn out with toil and hunger.

For ox-drawn carts downhill could be as difficult as uphill, especially for those carrying items such as horseshoes and nails. Another chronicler counted:

> 106 waggons drawn by four horses each, and 110 waggons each drawn by eight oxen, making a total of 424 horses and 880 oxen.

And the rest. Dere Street is traceable as its line runs through Midlothian (especially as it forms the main street of the village of Edgehead) and Edinburgh's modern suburbs, appearing to disappear around Nether Liberton, possibly at a crossing of the Braid Burn. It may have turned west there and aimed for the supply depot at Cramond. Built in 142AD, it used the River Almond as a natural anchorage where ships could unload goods for distribution to the forts along the eastern end of the Antonine Wall. Refortified in the early third century as a base for the invasion of the north by the Emperor Septimius Severus, its stone walls and gateways almost certainly survived into the early medieval period as a fortress for a Celtic warlord. Cramond Kirk was built much later on the site of the Roman fort's *principia*, the headquarters building, and there is a sense of the continuity of occupation at the mouth of the Almond. It made every sort of logistical sense for Edward II to continue marching on Dere Street if indeed it led to the gates of Cramond because the old depot lay much nearer to Stirling than the only other Roman alternative at Inveresk.

Having driven his men hard for three days, Edward awarded them a welcome respite as the army spent two days unloading supplies from the English fleet, the corn paid for by the cash borrowed from the Italian bankers and much else, and then reloading them into carts. This extended halt by the Forth also allowed the strung-out baggage train time to catch up. De Valence and his squadron had come across no resistance, no bands of mounted skirmishers lying in wait or attempting to harry stragglers, or at least none that were reported. But Robert Bruce had sent scouts to shadow Edward II's progress and they will have cantered back to the Tor Wood to report. Time was ticking and the English still had 30 miles to cover before they reached Stirling.

The terms of the truce brokered by Edward Bruce were unequivocal. If Edward II failed to approach within three miles of the castle by midsummer, Sir Philip Moubray was bound to open the gates to the Scots and surrender. King Robert could then have installed a garrison, supplied it generously and then melted into the western hills with his army intact. Having gained Stirling, what would be the point of risking open battle with such a numerically superior opponent? And numbers would tell in a different way, a way much more favourable to the Scots. Just as had happened in 1311, Edward would eventually have been forced to withdraw his hungry army – and nothing would have been achieved. It is therefore very surprising that at no point, or at least at no point that was recorded, did Bruce adopt his favoured tactics and dispatch small forces to attack and delay the English while they were marching against time and vulnerable.

Riders reported to King Robert that the English had once again formed up in marching order and early on Saturday, 22 June, they began to move west towards Stirling. The paramount need for speed would force them to take the fastest route possible, the Roman road to the line of the Antonine Wall where they could set up camp near Falkirk. The following day, Sunday, 23 June, they would then approach along the road from Camelon that led through the Tor Wood and the New Park. Where Bruce was waiting.

5
Bloody Sunday

The Eve of the Feast of St John the Baptist,
23rd day of June 1314.

At Watling Lodge in Falkirk, the ditch dug on the north side of the Antonine Wall is still remarkably well defined. Originally V-shaped and 40 feet across by at least 10 feet deep, it was in itself a formidable barrier. Although the ditch at Watling and Callendar Park now seems much wider at the bottom, that is a consequence of gravity, of centuries of infill. In 1314 the Roman wall will have been an even more impressive earthwork and in addition to its northern defences, the outline of its forts will also have been mostly upstanding.

The road that crossed the Antonine Wall at Watling Lodge led to the forward fort at Camelon. It was large and lay close to a point on the Carron Water which may have been navigable for the shallow draught of English supply ships. If such logistical coordination had been planned – and the English army contained several commanders who knew Scotland well – then the re-supply of the army at Camelon will have meant fewer wagons and a faster pace of march. The stretch between Edinburgh/Cramond and Falkirk/Camelon was demanding; at 25 miles the longest of the stages Edward's men had to complete. In addition to access, the Carron Water was also an abundant source of fresh water for a thirsty, hungry and exhausted army and its animals. For all these reasons, it may well be that when Edward II's captains called a halt in the evening of Saturday, 22 June, they planned to make use of the nearby Roman military engineering to corral their beasts and set up camp on the banks of the Carron.

If indeed pavilions were pitched and cooking fires lit inside the grassy ramparts, the fort will have made an appropriate setting for a council of war. Unless the Scots retreated – and there was always a likelihood – battle would be joined very soon. Plans needed to be laid. Unlike his father, Edward II was not a dominating figure, his personal appetites had diminished him and as his commanders gathered in the royal pavilion, there was a sense of the army slipping from the king's grasp. The ghost of Piers Gaveston stalked the camp at Camelon.

Four years before, Edward had been forced to agree to the appointment of 21 Lords Ordainers, a group of magnates and prelates chosen by a complex system of election. In the first parliament of the new reign, Gaveston had been named and criticised, and in 1309 the king was directly warned that if his favourite were not banished, there would be civil war. When the Ordainers issued an elaborate programme for the reform of government in 1311, these included an insistence that Gaveston would not return from exile. Overwhelmingly negative, the Ordinances ordained that the king could not grant any office, in central or local government, without the consent of parliament. Nor could he grant land, neither his own nor what was held of him in fee. The king could not leave the country or go to war and parliament would meet at least once a year, twice if necessary, to decide on matters of practicality and policy. Led by Robert Winchelsey, Archbishop of Canterbury, the Ordainers also sought control of the exchequer and insisted that Edward not borrow money, but 'live of his own'. These restrictions represented a stark contrast with the autocratic rule of his father. And after the murder of Gaveston in 1312, the biographer of the king summed up the nature of his relations with the great magnates: 'From that day a perpetual enmity grew up between the king and the earls.'

Once another medieval source, the *Lanercost Chronicle*, had concluded its own recital of this long-running dispute, there is a palpable sense of relief: 'And now,' wrote the compiler, 'let us return to Robert de Bruce and see what he has been up to in the meanwhile.'

Preparing a raid, was the answer. 'When Robert de Bruce heard of this discord in the south, he assembled a great army and invaded England [in 1312].' The Scots king was well aware of the tensions between Edward II and his nobles.

On the evening of Saturday, 22 June, it seems that these tensions bubbled to the surface once more. In the din and chaos of battle, when communications become scrambled or broken, decisiveness is crucial. One man, clearly in command, must be in a position to make quick decisions and those reporting to him must understand a clear chain of command. Dithering or no decision was often equivalent to a bad one. But in his plans for the coming battle, Edward II made the same fundamental error – twice.

Only three major magnates, three earls, came north in 1314 and two of them argued over the honour of commanding the vanguard, the fore-battle. This was an army in itself with around 600 armoured knights, 250 Welsh cavalry, 1,500 archers, 150 crossbowmen (many of them mercenaries) and 1,500 spearmen.

Gilbert de Clare, Earl of Gloucester, had remained close to Edward II throughout the time of the Ordainers and was his nephew, the son of Joan of Acre, Edward I's daughter. Inexperienced and only 24 years old, Gloucester nevertheless had a reputation for common sense. But perhaps because he had brought many retainers with him or because he scented glory, he insisted – or his uncle insisted – that he command the vanguard.

This was not acceptable to Humphrey de Bohun, Earl of Hereford. As Constable of England, he claimed that it was his right to lead and as one of the wealthiest magnates, he too had brought many well-armed followers to Scotland. In this circumstance the king should have set aside favour and made a clear and unequivocal decision, but instead he ducked it and appointed both Gloucester and Hereford as joint commanders of the vanguard. A cardinal failure of nerve and judgement, this compromise would prove costly.

Aymer de Valence must have shaken his head. The Earl of Pembroke, he was the most experienced of all, having fought Bruce twice, but instead he was given a lesser role as commander of about 200 knights in the main-battle. And with Sir Giles d'Argentan, he had the honour of riding beside the king, each man 'taking a rein' of the royal destrier as royal bodyguards and advisors. Perhaps de Valence had been nominated to take over command in the event that the king was killed. Edward himself led the main-battle, the centre of his army, where 800 or so knights would ride alongside 2,500 spearmen, the same number of archers and about 150 crossbowmen. And again the command structure saw some poor decision-making. The immensely experienced Sir Robert Clifford, a Northumbrian knight who knew Scotland and the Scots army well, was forced to share command of the cavalry of the main-battle with Sir Henry Beaumont, a cousin of the king. Beaumont's tactical naivety was soon made clear.

Meanwhile, to paraphrase the Lanercost chronicler, Robert

Bruce had no such difficulties. All of his commanders were seasoned soldiers, trusted to know their roles and trusted by their king. Having agreed to honeycomb the ground with pits or pots on either side of the Roman road at the Entry to the New Park, the Scots army had been formed up in retreat order. Guarding the Entry, where the road appears to have passed through woodland, was the rear-battle or the rearguard, commanded by King Robert. It was the largest of the three Scots battles, with four schiltrons of approximately 600 men in each. The decision to expose the king to what was likely to be the first assault by the English was surprising. As Edward did, kings usually led the centre of an army. It may be that Bruce placing himself and the largest battle at the Entry was a calculated risk. With the pots and their sharpened stakes funnelling the English into a narrow front, as had happened at Loudoun Hill, he could fight a limited engagement, give the armoured knights a bloody nose and then retreat. If that was indeed what was in the king's mind, it was a dangerous gambit since the mass of the English army lay behind their vanguard, including their deadly archers.

Beyond Bruce's battle were the two battles in the centre. One was commanded by his brother Edward and the other by James Douglas with the young Walter Stewart by his side. These were smaller, with three schiltrons of 600 men in each. The Scots vanguard lay beyond the main-battle, closest to Stirling and ready to lead the army north-west into the hills if a retreat were signalled. Thomas Randolph, Earl of Moray, led another three schiltrons of 600 men apiece. Around 1,500 archers had mustered in the New Park and at the head of a force of 500 or so light cavalry rode Sir Robert Keith.

Early in the morning of Sunday, 23 June, the gates of Stirling Castle were unbarred and swung open. Probably with a squire riding at his side, Sir Philip Moubray clattered over the drawbridge and down the main street of the little town clustered on the eastern tail of the castle rock. Almost certainly in receipt of a safe-conduct from King Robert, the governor of the castle made his way south towards Camelon and the English camp. He probably skirted the Scots positions by riding in a western arc before finding the hard standing of the Roman road. King Edward's army was already on the march and when Moubray met the knights of the vanguard, he asked to see their king urgently.

Observing the letter of the truce, he told Edward that without striking a blow or risking a single soldier, he had already fulfilled its conditions because his forces would reach within three miles of Stirling. That meant the castle was technically relieved and did not have to be surrendered. More than that, said Moubray, the Scots were in a strong position in the New Park and were difficult to outflank because they had made the woods on either side of the Entry impassable by blocking the paths. And since no mention of them troubling the English cavalry has survived, the pots and their sharpened stakes on either side of the road may also have been reported to King Edward by his governor. There was no need to fight, insisted Moubray, the Scots were formed up for flight and might well melt away into the west once they had seen the strength of the army coming to meet them.

Very little, if any, of this valuable advice and intelligence seems to have been communicated to the vanguard. Or if a galloper was got away to inform the earls of Gloucester and Hereford, he was ignored. Perhaps they had passed Moubray on the road as he sought out the king, but even so there was plenty of time to share the information between that meeting in the morning and the events that unfolded much later in the evening. And distances were not disabling. Perhaps confidence in the English camp was so high that whatever the Scots had done or prepared, victory felt inevitable. The omens were good.

On the march from Camelon, Edward's knights and infantry had passed close to a remarkable piece of Roman architecture. Known as Arthur's O'On, it was a temple that had stood virtually intact until 1743 when a local landowner demolished it so that he could use the squared-off stone to build a mill-dam on the River Carron. Circular, beehive or oven-shaped, 'the temple beside Camelon' was noted in the early 1300s when Edward I was busy destroying Scottish antiquities. On condition that sculptures and inscriptions were removed, the Hammer of the Scots and destroyer of their history, allowed Arthur's O'On to stand. It was probably a triumphal monument raised to celebrate a Roman victory. Perhaps the English vanguard trotted past it in eager anticipation of another victory over the Scots.

That outcome may have seemed all too likely to James Douglas and Sir Robert Keith when they led a small scouting party south out of the New Park to discover the strength, disposition and rate of advance of the English army. They rode quickly back to report to Bruce that a huge and well-equipped army was approaching fast up the Roman road. John Barbour put words in their mouths

> . . . so many braided banners, standards and spear pennons, and so many mounted knights all flaming in gay attire, and so many broad battles taking such vast space as they rode, as might, by their number and

> battle array, have dismayed the greatest and boldest and best host in Christendom.

The king told Douglas and Keith to lie. So that their confidence was not dented, the Scots army was told that the English were marching towards their well-drilled and well-organised ranks in 'ill array'.

As the vanguard moved north from Camelon/Falkirk, their pennants fluttering in the summer breeze, the Scots in the New Park made their own preparations. Sunday, 23 June, was the eve of the Feast of St John the Baptist and as men knelt on the grass, their heads bowed, priests said mass and summoned God's help and blessing for the day to come. It is easily forgotten that religious belief was absolute in the fourteenth century and because the Scots were certain that their cause was just, almost all will have been equally certain that God would come to the New Park and stand beside them. And if they died in the battle to come, they would die in His sight, their souls shriven and commended to Him in the mass said on that summer Sunday morning.

Most chroniclers, like the Lanercost compiler, were clerics with the benefit of hindsight, and they contrasted the simple piety of the Scots and their king with Edward II's disregard for the proprieties. There is also a whiff of disapproval for a man who appears not to have troubled to hide his homosexuality. In the march north it was reported that the English king failed to be respectful of the saints, but the most notorious transgression took place much earlier, in 1306. Edward I wished to formally knight his son at Westminster Abbey and brought together a glittering gathering of magnates to witness this chivalric rite of passage for the heir to the throne. Two hundred and sixty-seven other young men were to be knighted at the same time. But instead of spending the night before the ceremony in prayer and fasting, Edward of Caernarvon embarked on a drunken spree with his friends, including Piers Gaveston.

Once the sober Scottish schiltrons had been blessed in the New Park, they ate a simple breakfast, probably oatcakes or bread washed down with cold water from one of the burns. With his commanders, Bruce rode to the Entry to see that all had been done properly in the digging of the pots, the placing of sharpened stakes and the covering over with brackens, twigs and grass. Six hundred years later, in 1923, in the anaerobic conditions of Milton Bog, not far from the Entry, the preserved remains of sharpened wooden stakes were discovered. Tangible footnotes to history. When the king was satisfied that preparations were complete, he had his army assembled in the New Park. Perhaps he was thoughtful, gathering himself for what was to come. It seems that Bruce believed that the armies would clash that day.

Battlefield speeches from commanders were traditional but also difficult. When an army was large and spread over a wide front, heralds were used to repeat the royal exhortations, but on Sunday, 23 June, King Robert may have been able to make himself heard to all of his men gathered by the fringes of the woodland. Dressed in a surcoat blazoned with the royal arms and with a gold circlet on his helm but not wearing all of his battle armour and on a pony rather than a warhorse, Bruce rode up and down the lines. John Barbour recorded – or more likely embellished – these words:

> Whatsoever man found his heart not assured to stand and win all, and to maintain that mighty struggle or die with honour, should betimes leave the field, and

> that none should remain but those who would stand
> by him to the end, and take the fortune God sent.

At about the same time as Bruce was summoning up real, or Barbour's imagined, eloquence, Edward II was being armoured by his squires and helped into the saddle of his destrier. Wedged tight by the high pommel and cantle, a knight could be difficult to unhorse if he could distribute his great weight correctly and use his legs as aids for his horse. But mail, armour and weaponry were very heavy, needing real strength to carry and at the same time retain reasonable movement. Knights were used to spending long and weary hours sweating inside all that metal and exhaustion as much as courage and skill could be determinant in hand-to-hand combat. And since Stirling was not far, only 10 miles from the camp at Camelon/Falkirk, most men will have been fully armoured from early in the morning of Sunday, 23 June.

Their destriers were also meticulously turned out. After muck and mud had been picked out of their feet and their shoes checked – a loose or lost shoe could unbalance a horse and make its paces disunited – each was 'barded' or armoured. And it may be that all were mounted for the ride north, certainly those in the vanguard will have been on their warhorses and not palfreys or ponies. Squires, sergeants and other attendants carried lances and other gear until the moment of need came.

Of all the riders and soldiers of Edward II's army, one contingent was probably thought to hold the balance of power, the ability to change the course of the battle with Bruce. For more than a century after 1314, English archery dominated warfare in western Europe and the secrets of that remarkable dominance were revealed in an unlikely discovery.

The wreck of Henry VIII's great warship, the *Mary Rose*, was found in 1971 on the bed of the Solent, the straits to the north of the Isle of Wight. Raised in 1982, the ship was found to contain many archaeological treasures. One of the most fascinating was a cache of 137 English longbows and more than 3,500 arrows. This was a signal moment in understanding the history of medieval warfare. Because of wear and tear and the organic nature of the objects, no bows and arrows had survived from before the end of the fifteenth century and those late examples were very few and precious.

There were enough bows found on the *Mary Rose* to allow some to be rigorously tested, even to destruction. These experiments showed something very simple. What gave medieval English archers their extraordinary dominance was sheer strength, the ability to pull the bowstring of a very long bow back to such a tremendous degree that it sent arrows high into the air over long distances with great accuracy. This is known as draw-weight and it is measured in pounds-force. A modern longbow has a draw-weight of about 60 pounds-force, pulling the bowstring back 28 inches. The actor Robert Hardy wrote a superb account of the history of the longbow and he estimated the original draw-weights of the bows from the *Mary Rose* was much higher, at between 150 pounds-force and 160 pounds-force, pulling the bowstring back 30 inches. The full range of draw-weights of the bows was found to be between 100 pounds-force and 185 pounds-force. There are very few modern bowmen who can achieve this. As it marched to Stirling, the army of Edward II had 6,500 men who could all exert this huge power, and do it in the heat of battle.

It was not only the case that men who worked all year as farmers, without the aid of machinery and in all weathers, had far greater upper body strength, it was also a question of technique. Writing towards the end of the fifteenth century, here is Hugh Latimer describing how boys trained to be archers:

> [My father] taught me how to draw, how to lay my body in my bow . . . not to draw with strength of arms as divers other nations do . . . I had my bows bought me according to my age and strength, as I increased in them, so my bows were made bigger and bigger. For men shall never shoot well unless they be brought up to it . . .

What Latimer was describing is difficult to visualise but in essence, it involved using his body weight to push with his left arm and the left hand that gripped the bow while pulling back the bowstring with his right. Bending the bow instead of only drawing the bowstring.

Archers needed to be able to keep up a rapid rate of fire – but without exhausting themselves. Arrows were supplied to them in sheaves of 24 and for speed of use were stabbed into the ground in front of each man. The muck on the metal tip might also have the side-effect of causing infection if it hit its mark. Medieval archers could be recognised by their skeletons. Their left arms, the one extended to hold the bowstave, were enlarged and bone spurs or osteophytes are often found on their left wrists, left shoulders and right fingers. These were caused by inflammation through over-use and they are clinical evidence of the technique of archery described by Hugh Latimer. From boyhood archers practised in the butts, honing their skills, developing their deadly muscle-power for the battlefield as their bodies adapted.

Bows were usually made from close-grained, slow-growing woods such as yew or box. They had great strength and elasticity, and were unlikely to snap in the hands of a strong archer. The demand for yew in the fourteenth century was so great that domestic stocks became very depleted and supplies had to be imported from Europe. Those staves taken from the *Mary Rose* deserved the description of longbows for they average 6 foot 6 inches in length. When the archers of Edward II marched up the Roman road in the summer of 1314 they carried their bows unstrung, and at a distance may have resembled spearmen. When they reached the Tor Wood, their captains may have signalled bows to be strung. This involved attaching a loop of bowstring (made from flax, hemp or even silk – and most archers carried spare strings, often under their hats to keep them warm and flexible) to a horned nock attached to the lower tip of the stave and then bending it so that they could loop it over the top nock or notch.

So many arrows were needed in battle that wagons filled with sheaves of 24 trundled up the north road alongside the men who would send them flying into the sky. Unlike spears or pike-shafts, arrows could not be made from naturally growing sapling wood and then simply seasoned. To fly far and true, arrows had to be arrow-straight. This meant production on a semi-industrial scale. Usually made from poplar but also ash or beech, all trees that grew tall and straight with good grain, arrows were made by a process of splitting and re-splitting young trees. Poplars grow quickly and an arrowsmith would cut a tree, brash off its limbs and then saw it into sections approximately 30 to 36 inches in length. And then with a series of splitters known as draw-knives, he divided and redivided each section until the required gauge or thickness was achieved. Each arrow-length was then rounded with abrasives to make it aerodynamic by smoothing off the split edges. Fletchers preferred goose feathers and attached them with natural glue and thin cord. At the business end, a metal arrowhead was fitted, with the short bodkin being the classic design. At the other end perhaps the most fiddly job was to attach a notched horn nock. This was very important because the draw-weight was so great that when released the bowstring could have otherwise split the arrow. The volumes turned out by England's arrowsmiths and fletchers were vast. Between 1341 and 1359 royal armies used 51,350 sheaves or 1,232,400 arrows.

When they reached the New Park, Edward II's archers would have been disappointed. Because of their great strength and skill, they could fire accurately and quickly at a range of more than 350 yards. The quilted jackets of the Scottish spearmen supplied scant protection and specially cut heavy war arrows, like small javelins, could pierce chain mail and even armour when fired at point-blank range with maximum draw-weight. Often archers aimed at destriers to bring them down but if an arrow pierced armour, it could be agony as a knight rode across uneven ground with its point held fast as it lacerated his body, the movement of the horse causing it to score his body like a long stylus. But these thoughts may not have been at the front of archers' mind when they saw the woodland. Trees made good shelter from volleys and there appeared to be little open ground for longer-range work.

Archers had turned the battle at Falkirk in 1298 when they had badly depleted the ranks of the schiltrons before the Scots spearmen were blown away by an armoured cavalry charge. And at the battle of Halidon Hill near Berwick in 1333, the arrows fell like deadly rain and the Scots army was destroyed. Surely there would be a chance for these remarkable soldiers to bend their backs and send death into the sky at Stirling. But not if Robert Bruce could help it.

As they rode and marched through a medieval landscape devoid of the noise of machines, where all the background sounds were the sounds of nature, the weather, the chatter and song of birds, the lowing of animals, an army of 14,000 men, their horses, oxen and wagons could be heard for miles around. The low, rhythmic tramp of thousands of feet shuddered through the summer air and the droning hum of many voices grew louder and louder. By the late afternoon of Sunday, 23 June, the Scots rearguard could see as well as hear the English approaching. From his position at the Entry, King Robert watched the bright surcoats and fluttering standards of their vanguard ride out of the Tor Wood from precisely the direction he had predicted. In what reads as a very credible piece of reporting, John Barbour had Bruce outline his reason for choosing the ground at the New Park:

> The enemy are bound to try to pass through the New Park, unless they go below us across the marsh [the boggy carseland towards the Forth]. Thus, either way, we shall be at an advantage. On foot, among the trees, we shall get the better of mounted men; alternatively, the sikes [of the carseland] will put their cavalry out of action.

But then, just as it seemed that all was going to plan, confusion and surprise almost turned Bruce's calculation upside down.

As they neared the Bannock Burn and could at last see Stirling Castle on its great rock, the vanguard of the English army (in itself about half the size of the entire Scottish army) appeared to have moved far ahead of Edward II and the main battle and lost contact with them. It seems that the king and his commanders, the experienced Aymer de Valence amongst them, were debating whether or not to halt and make camp somewhere near the southern edges of the Tor Wood. It was late afternoon and men and animals would soon become weary.

But up ahead the cavalry under Gloucester and Hereford knew nothing of this proposal. John Barbour wrote: '. . . the vanguard knew nothing of this halt and delay and rode with good array, without stopping, straight to the Park'. As they pushed on, all was excitement and exhilaration. When the riders at the front of the vanguard reached Snabhead, on the southern ridge above the shallow valley of the Bannock Burn, they caught their first sight of the enemy. Across the burn, less than a mile away, it seemed to the English that the Scots spearmen were behaving true to form, retreating, running with some urgency. It is very likely that the vanguard of mounted knights and other cavalry approached the Entry much more quickly than Bruce anticipated. And to the impetuous riders in the van of the vanguard, it may have looked as though their march against time had been for nothing, as though the Scots were yet again refusing to fight. Desperate for battle, desperate to engage, many dug in their spurs, roared on their destriers and galloped towards glory across the Bannock Burn.

Most of this charging squadron were retainers of the Earl of Hereford, joint commander of the vanguard, and his nephew, Sir Henry de Bohun, was certainly amongst them. Less hotheaded than the rest, it may be that de Bohun halted the headlong charge so that instead of a disorganised mêlée, they could mount a close-formation advance that could break into a concerted charge. As they closed on the Scots, the riders perhaps realised that the enemy was not retreating but falling quickly into the ranks of the schiltron. It may also be the case that the English cavalry knew of the existence of the pots, the leg-breaking, leaf and grass-covered pits that had been dug on either side of the Roman road. No mention is made of them by any of the sources as they describe the events that began to unfold.

Once de Bohun had reined in his men, he looked over to the Scottish lines. They had indeed formed up into a schiltron, their spear-points bristling as the sun began to dip in the early evening. According to one chronicler, it was 'after dinner' when de Bohun rode up to the Entry of the New Park. As his men and their horses drew breath, the young English knight noticed something that dismissed all of his caution. Riding up and down in front of the ranks of the Scottish schiltron on a grey pony was a man who wore a surcoat with the royal lion of Scotland sewn on it. He was not fully armoured and had only a hand axe at his belt. But around his helmet there seemed to be a circlet of gold. Was this Robert Bruce, the usurper king, the commander of the Scottish army?

Dreams of glory filled de Bohun's heart, a battle won before it was begun, adrenalin pumped through his veins and he wheeled his destrier towards the Scots' lines. If he was able to make out the circlet of gold on Bruce's bassinet, the English knight cannot have been much more than 150 yards from him. Gripping his lance, he kicked on his snorting warhorse and began to trot, canter and then quickly break into the gallop. If at that moment Bruce had had his back turned as he talked to his troops, they could see what thundered towards him and will have screamed warnings.

The king was indeed not fully armoured, only on a pony and carried only an axe. His captains will have roared for him not to expose himself but to ride quickly back behind the ranks of the schiltron. But he did not listen.

When Bruce turned his little grey to see de Bohun galloping towards him, his lance couched and levelled, he had only seconds to react. And what then happened was a testament to extraordinary bravery, skill and horsemanship. If a charging knight holds a shield in one arm and a lance in the other hand, he is forced to drop his reins. That means his control over his horse is much diminished for he can use only his legs and his seat to direct it. Bruce knew that. And so all that de Bohun could hope to do was keep his destrier at the gallop and in a straight line. Without reins, he could not easily make the horse change direction. Bruce knew that too.

As the hoofbeats kicked up dust and earth and drummed towards him, Bruce waited. And did not move. He saw that de Bohun's lance had to be aimed on one side of the destrier's neck and that it would be difficult for him to swing its point over the horse's head quickly if Bruce suddenly moved to the offside. In the mind of an experienced medieval cavalry warrior, these were not calculations or matters of conscious thought but pure instinct. And so when de Bohun was only yards away, almost on him, his lance-point searching for Bruce's unarmoured breast, the king neck-reined his little pony to one side, the opposite side from the Englishman's lance. The pony fiddled his feet and as John Barbour pithily noted: 'Schir Henry missit the nobill kyng'. As de Bohun began to pass him, Bruce had to stand up in his stirrups of his little horse and with a back-handed stroke, he brought the axe down on the knight's helmeted head.

Most of the sources insist that with only a short-handled

axe, Bruce's blow had sufficient force to shear through the steel of his enemy's helmet and his skull, killing him instantly. That may indeed be exactly what happened and the force was so great that the handle of the axe broke, but it is much more likely that the back-handed stroke cut through chain mail and into the much softer tissue of de Bohun's neck. Which could also have killed him instantly. In any case, this remarkable and famous incident seemed to set the tone for all of the events that followed. Bruce's commanders were rightly angry that the king had risked himself in this way – but they had no time to remonstrate. The pace of events began to quicken.

It seems that as de Bohun charged the king, the main body of the vanguard was catching up fast. In a touching snapshot moment of chivalry, the English knight's squire stood over his master's body to protect it from being hacked at, defiled or looted. But the boy was swept away and killed as the Scots schiltron surged forward. Avoiding the honeycomb of pots on either side of the road, the English cavalry under the joint command of the earls of Hereford and Gloucester formed up and charged the pikemen. But all seemed confusion and ill order. No archers were deployed to fire volleys into the dense ranks of the schiltrons, presumably because their own cavalry was engaged and in danger of being hit by friendly fire. It may be that the pots did indeed succeed in funnelling the front of the charging knights and making them ineffective. Gloucester had his horse killed from under him or was hooked and pulled off it by pikemen, but he was dragged clear of capture. In what seems to have been a ferocious if limited engagement, Edward Bruce may have led his schiltron through the trees of the New Park to reinforce his brother's men.

It was now early evening but the English fought on for some time, apparently in the belief that the Scots still planned to retreat. And so they needed to do as much damage as they could to Bruce's small army. But then, at a signal from their captains, the armoured cavalry began to pull back and withdraw, splashing across the Bannock Burn. Sensing that they could punch home a real advantage, the Scots pikemen began to pursue, but it is a testament to their discipline that Bruce was able to recall them back to their position at the Entry.

This incident speaks of surprise on the part of the Scots and a chaotic chain of command with the English. Since he was not armoured, not on his warhorse and armed only with a small battle axe, it seems that Bruce was caught unawares by the speed of the English advance. In the heat of a famous moment in history, he risked everything as his warrior's instincts overcame his usual caution. But the sight of their king cutting down a charging English knight only yards from where they stood must have made Scots morale sing and put belief in the hearts of those that were wavering. And the fact that they drove back the armoured flower of English chivalry might have convinced many that their time might have come and that all that drilling and training might at last tell.

Chaos appeared to have clouded English tactics. Edward II did not order the vanguard to begin hostilities and attack the Scots. In fact it was so late in the day that he was considering making camp. And he cannot have been made aware of what happened until much later. In their turn, the earls of Gloucester and Hereford probably did not know that a second cavalry engagement took place on that evening of Sunday, 23 June.

From a vantage point at the Entry, King Robert had seen a

second English squadron riding northwards. It looked as though they were taking a wide arc around the edge of the New Park, following a bridle path that became known as the Way. Led by Sir Robert Clifford and Sir Henry Beaumont, this force was probably only 300 or so strong, not large, but it seemed to Bruce that it was intent on something he had planned to avoid. Having stationed the schiltron of Thomas Randolph, Earl of Moray, as his vanguard around St Ninian's Kirk on the road to Stirling, he intended it to bar that road and prevent his army from being outflanked. And preserve the option of retreating. Even as late as Sunday evening, the English still appeared to believe that the Scots would indeed retreat and it may be that the principal purpose of Clifford's tactic was to block that option. It is also likely that Gloucester and Hereford were unaware of this manoeuvre, and that Edward II, far to the rear, was not aware of anything that was happening up ahead.

For some reason Thomas Randolph was with Bruce at the Entry when the king saw Clifford's squadron moving out wide and he rebuked his commander in a quaint phrase, something not likely to have been said in the heat of battle at a moment when the Scottish strategy was looking as though it might collapse. 'A rose had fallen from his chaplet', was what Bruce said, according to John Barbour, when he accused Moray of blundering in allowing the English to outflank them. A chaplet is an antique term for a garland. Apparently stung by this genteel rebuke, Randolph rode back quickly to St Ninian's Kirk and arrived just in time to lead his schiltron out of the woods to confront Clifford and the English cavalry. What happened next turned out to be determinant.

The sharp fight between Clifford and Beaumont's squadron and Randolph's schiltron formed a central part of the account of

Bannockburn in the *Scalachronica* because it was there that Sir Thomas Grey's father charged the Scottish ranks in an act of rash bravery. By the time the English had circled round towards St Ninian's Kirk, only a mile or so from Stirling Castle, they still had open ground to cross. And when the Scots emerged from the trees to form up and bar the way, Sir Henry Beaumont said, 'Let them come on, give them some ground. We must draw back a little.' Oozing confidence, he was looking to create space, enough ground for a squadron of armoured knights to draw together into a line, knee to knee, and then kick their destriers into a charge that would have real momentum. Sir Thomas Grey was sceptical: 'My lord, give them what you like now; I'm afraid that in a short while, they will have everything.'

It was a curious remark, as though Grey expected defeat, or simply thought that the ground or the circumstances were not suitable. This exchange quickly degenerated into a squabble as the destriers pawed at the ground, anticipating the gallop. 'Flee then,' snapped Beaumont, 'flee if you're afraid!' It was the sort of insult no knight could tolerate and Grey immediately dug into his horse's flanks and with Sir William Deyncourt galloping at his side, charged the spears of the schiltron. It was a mad, impetuous and useless gesture that must have given the Scots immense confidence. Deyncourt was killed at once and Grey's horse stabbed to a writhing, squealing death by pikes. And then in a tactic that cannot have been uncommon, 'shooters' ran out from the ranks of the schiltron and dragged Sir Thomas Grey behind them to make him a prisoner who would later fetch a lucrative ransom. And also live to give an account of the events of that Sunday, 23 June, to his son. Barbour wrote of soldiers, probably armed with pikes that carried axe-heads at their tips instead of points. Known as Jeddart or Lochaber axes, they were used by men who 'shoot out of their formation, stab horses . . . and bring men down'.

Extremely limited in his tactical abilities, all that Sir Henry Beaumont could think to do was to launch repeated and increasingly futile charges against the tightly packed spearmen. He had brought no archers with him even though the Scots were fighting on open ground and not sheltered by the woodland. Holding tight together, the Scots repulsed all of Beaumont's assaults, stabbing at the destriers to try to bring them down. So frustrated were the English horsemen that they threw their weapons at the Scots – swords, maces and axes – because their lances were useless, too short to penetrate the spiky hedge of ten- and twelve-foot spears. And as the Scots roared defiance, many destriers will have spooked and swerved away. The noise of the battle at St Ninian's Kirk must have been intense but intermittent as Beaumont's cavalry broke off to re-form to charge again.

Watching from the woods were King Robert and James Douglas. When it became clear that the discipline of the Scots would hold and that no archers were being brought up, Bruce held Douglas back from reinforcing Randolph. It was late and the light must have begun to fade as the sun dipped behind the Ochils. And Bruce may have been anxious not to over-commit his forces or risk more men in a fight that was in any case turning Randolph's way. That evening there had been attacks at two points, the Entry and at the kirk. Perhaps another assault would be launched. It was also an issue of morale and chivalry. If the schiltron could beat back the squadron of armoured knights without help, then glory would be theirs and the morale of the whole army would again be lifted.

And they did hold. The light faded, the English tired and

the Scots slowly advanced, dispersing Clifford and Beaumont's cavalry. Some retreated south on the Way, the bridle path they had followed, while others rode north for the sanctuary of Stirling Castle. It was a signal moment. When the English abandoned the fight, Moray's schiltron was exultant, exhilarated and exhausted. Their comrades congratulated them and their king smiled. They had shown that spearmen could prevail over armoured knights on open ground – so long as there were no archers.

In the half-darkness of the night of 23 June there would be no more fighting, although events would take place that would profoundly influence what happened when morning came.

Hindsight blinds an understanding of how history shifts, sometimes hour by hour. Because Bannockburn was won, it is an easy assumption that, buoyed up by their king's killing of de Bohun, the failure of the English vanguard at the Entry and the scattering of Clifford and Beaumont's squadron at St Ninian's Kirk, the morale of the Scots would have been soaring sky-high, many of the pikemen full of confidence that they could inflict a crushing defeat. By contrast, camped amongst the pools and sikes of the carseland, exhausted after a long march, the English must have been downcast, lacking belief, full of foreboding for the day to come.

On the night of Sunday, 23 June, as the simmer dim crept across the Forth Valley, none of these tidy assumptions are likely to have been accurate. Few in the English army, including the king, saw what happened to de Bohun, Gloucester, Hereford, Clifford and Beaumont. And few had even seen the Scots army, far less developed a fear that they would be overcome by them, whoever they were. Instead, rumour probably ricocheted around the camp on the carse as men tended cooking fires, sorted their gear and tried to find a dry place to lie for a few hours of snatched sleep. Sir Thomas Grey later told his son that the English army 'remained all night in discomfort, being mortified and badly troubled by the events of the previous day'. But that night he was already a prisoner of the Scots and had no first-hand testimony to offer. In fact, mixed with hindsight, his own predicament must have coloured his recollection deeply.

The New Park was small, only a mile from the Entry to St Ninian's Kirk and two miles from east to west. Taking into account the extent of the carseland, it is striking how many men were packed into such a small area. There can be no doubt that the sounds of that fateful night carried clear across the half-dark. As their fires twinkled, the armies could hear each other, the murmur of conversation and preparation occasionally punctuated by a shout or the snort and whinny of skittish, spooking horses. From the higher ground of the New Park and its sheltering woodland, Robert Bruce's commanders could both see and hear their enemies in the carse below as their council of war began.

Somewhere amongst the trees, in a clearing where an awning could be guyed, the Scots king had summoned his captains. Some were men who had been at his side since the early, fragile days after the coronation at Scone, soldiers such as the dashing James Douglas, his brother Edward and the loyal Aonghas Og Macdonald. Others had joined the Bruce cause later: Thomas Randolph, Robert Keith, while others were there because their families and lands were important, like Walter Stewart. And as the king's constant councillor, Abbot Bernard of Arbroath was almost certainly present. He had brought with him to Bannockburn the Brecbennoch, the ancient reliquary that held some sacred remains of St Columba. Its power was said to be great and inspirational, especially for the Gaels in the Scots army.

As the council reviewed the events of the day, Randolph no doubt still flushed with relief and triumph at his victory at the kirk, it is likely that they rebuked the king for the outrageous and unnecessary risk he took in confronting Sir Henry de Bohun. All could have been lost in a single moment. Brave, charismatic, even regal, Bruce was utterly central to the great enterprise all of them had joined, risking their lives and their lands. The king was irreplaceable. Perhaps Edward Bruce raised an eyebrow at that, but all his brother could say was that he had broken the shaft of his good axe.

That night in the woods of the New Park two fundamental options presented themselves: fight or flight. The army was still drawn up in retreat order, they had inflicted some damage on the English, their own casualties had been light, and so large was Edward's army that, as in 1311, it would soon be forced to retreat, hungry and frustrated. According to the *Scalachronica*, the more favoured option before the council was to strike camp, and leave the New Park immediately under cover of night so that in the morning the English would wake to find themselves without an adversary.

> The Scots in the wood thought they had done well enough for the day, and were on the point of decamping in order to march during the night into the Lennox, a stronger country.

Support for this cautious, prudent course of action was strengthened by bad news. Word came across the River Forth from Cambuskenneth Abbey, which stood to the east of Stirling, of a massacre. Under the command of Sir William Airth, a small detachment guarded the Scots' supplies in the church precincts. But on the night of 23 June they were attacked by the forces of David de Strathbogie, the Earl of Atholl, a magnate whose father had been loyal to Bruce and present at Scone in 1306. Dishonour and betrayal may have been the motives, for it seems that Edward Bruce and Atholl's sister, Isabella, had had a son together. But instead of marrying her, he appears to have become betrothed to Isabella de Ross. The attack on Cambuskenneth and the massacre of Airth and his men may have reinforced Bruce's instincts to withdraw into the Lennox, the wilds of Bannauc. Especially if supplies were running short.

In the midge-infested carseland where his retinue had set up Edward II's royal pavilion, caution does not seem to have been in the air. On a warm midsummer night, over the damp sikes and boggy pools, clouds of midges must have made life uncomfortable for men and animals alike. Rather, rancour seems to have infected discussion as Edward brought his commanders together.

At what must have been a fractious council of war, when ill-temper simmered and sometimes boiled over, Sir Ingram de Umfraville, a Scot loyal to Edward and an experienced soldier who had once been a Guardian of the Realm of Scotland, proposed a potentially crazy plan. He suggested that the English army should pretend to withdraw, abandoning their camp and all manner of valuable gear. The Scots would then be tempted into a trap – and then the English would turn and pounce. The king rejected it out of hand as unworkable. And in any event, after all the frustrations of the retreat of 1311, did he not have in front of him a Scots army that might at last fight? There could be only one outcome of a pitched battle.

The Earl of Gloucester argued delay. The army was in such disarray, ploutering about in the bogs of the carse, that surely it made sense to take a day to organise the English forces properly. Many had not crossed the Bannock Burn, and contact with their captains cannot have been secure. But the idea of delay enraged the king and in front of all his councillors he accused Gilbert de Clare of cowardice. The Earl of Hereford cannot have been unable to resist a smile. No doubt de Clare and the king glared at each other and such continuing antipathy would reap a fatal reward the following day. It was not a productive council of war and if any plan other than all-out attack was agreed, it would be difficult to discern what it was in the battle that followed.

As for Hugh Despenser, probably Edward II's lover, he had brought his furniture to the bogs of Bannockburn and was very unwilling to see it lugged south again. Despenser's enthusiasm for the fight and the prize of the poorly furnished earldom of Moray may have been influential with the king who, at least earlier that day, may have been inclined to delay until his whole army could be brought properly together. But what is certain is that Edward cannot have been anything other than furious at the reckless free-lancing of his vanguard commanders. Any command structure that had been in place had fractured and no doubt with the support of Aymer de Valence and Sir Giles d'Argentan, he attempted to reassert his authority. Events were to show that he failed.

Beyond the royal pavilion, soldiers pokered up their cooking fires, hoping that the smoke would help keep the midgies manageable. In contrast to the arguments raging in the royal council, it seems that the blunders and confusions of the day had done little to dent their morale. They had not seen Gloucester unhorsed or Clifford driven off. Indeed, there is some slight evidence that their confidence was high. That part of the baggage train that carried barrels of ale and cider must have caught up and crossed the Bannock Burn because the Scots could hear the unmistakable sounds of drinking and merriment coming up from the camp in the carse. One chronicler recorded shouts of *Wassail!* and *Drinkhail!* These are medieval toasts and they will have been well known to the men of the Earl of Gloucester in particular since *wassail* was a reference to cider. Songs were sung as cups were downed, and the 'Gloucester Wassail' is perhaps the most famous:

> Wassail! Wassail! All over the town
> Our toast it is white and our ale it is brown.

As the soldiers caroused and the night wore on, a man slipped unseen out of the English camp. Under cover of darkness, he carefully made his way towards the New Park. No doubt looking over his shoulder at the pickets set by his comrades, the fugitive had to make the dangerous crossing of no-man's-land before encountering the challenge of those set as lookouts by Bruce's captains. Certainly the English were wary of a night attack and after the debâcle at Methven, Bruce will never have failed to instruct that sentries be posted. When he reached the Scottish lines, this man's accent and nationality may have helped him persuade whomever he encountered that he had to see the king without delay. In the *Scalachronica*, Sir Thomas Grey takes up the story:

> . . . when Sir Alexander de Seton, who was in the service of England and had come thither with the king, secretly left the English army, went to Robert de Brus in the wood and said to him: 'Sir, this is the time

> if you ever undertake to reconquer Scotland. The English have lost heart and are discouraged, and expect nothing but a sudden, open attack.' Then he described their condition, and pledged his head, on pain of being hanged and drawn, that if he [Bruce] would attack them on the morrow he would defeat them easily without [much] loss.

Now, Seton had attended the coronation at Scone in 1306 and changed sides at least twice, and his intervention will have been treated with some caution, but nevertheless, his words appeared to turn the tide of opinion. Bruce and his captains knew that the ground favoured them. The English had been forced to camp in a narrow, awkward and damp place and the drier ground between the carse and the New Park was also restricted by the Bannock Burn on one side and the Pelstream Burn on the other. The events of the day had shown clearly that there was confusion and dissent amongst the leadership of the army, and Edward's authority appeared to be crumbling. Seton's report had reinforced those impressions. Was it now or never? The one factor that no doubt troubled the Scots king was something he could not predict. What part would the English archers play? If he could engage his schiltrons quickly with the English and use the dangers of friendly fire to neutralise them, the battle by the Bannock Burn might turn his way.

As the toasts and the songs of the soldiers camped on the carselands died away into a fitful silence, the sun began to climb behind the Ochil Hills. A new day was dawning.

6

Black Monday

Vigils. The Feast of the Nativity of St John the Baptist, in the Year of Our Lord, 1314, the eighth year of the reign of Robert, first of that name, King of Scotland, Lord of Man.

The sun was rising over the Ochils away to the north-east and as its yellow glow melted down the flanks of the hills, the warming glint of the Forth meandered below Stirling Castle rock and a day dawned that would make a nation. By 4am it was light enough to see, to make out more than the grey shapes of the half-dark night moving around the English camp in the carseland below. Those men who had managed a few hours of fitful sleep roused, scratched, stretched and shook off the stiffness of their damp beds before looking for somewhere to relieve themselves. Many will have done no more than doze, knowing what was to come in the morning. Squires and pages will have slept very little as they attended tethered destriers, always alert even when the war-horses stilled and slept a little, their eyes flickering shut, bottom lips loose. Many had been tacked up and bitted all through the night, fearful of a surprise Scots attack, and few will have buckled their legs and sighed down to the ground to sleep. As the great beasts snuffled at what little forage their grooms could find, their riders began to wake and bark out orders for help to armour themselves. Around the royal pavilions messengers scurried off with orders for the great magnates and their retinues to make ready. Farriers moved amongst the destriers, nails and shoes in the pouches of their leather aprons, clawed hammers in their hands.

Occasionally a squire would raise a hand and a clench-nail would be driven home and bent over to grip the hoof tight.

Archers bent their backs in the cool of the morning, flexed and stretched their arms and made certain of spare bowstrings. Each man walked to the carts and took a sheaf of 24 arrows. A warm and sunny day was dawning – and in the early stillness there seemed not to be a breath of wind. If the weather held fair and fine, death might rain down from the skies and the Scots would fall in their hundreds, maybe thousands, on this midsummer day. Infantrymen looked for their spears and helmets, pulling the laces of their padded jackets tight and cinching their belts. All of the men who had bivouacked on the damp carse looked for water, especially those who had wassailed in the short night, and all chewed on dry bread and perhaps a morsel of hard cheese. It was the Feast of St John the Baptist and on holy days good Christians ate frugally – and on the morning of battle, at the outset of a day when many men would meet their maker, all soldiers were good Christians. Thoughtful sergeants took something out to the pickets who had been set on the edge of the carseland, men who looked towards the dark woods of the New Park and the Scots camp.

Moving through the trees, rousing their men with a nudge or even a kick, the decurions began to gather their section of their schiltron, checking that each man carried all of his kit and knew where to muster. Following the council of war of the night before, word had spread like wildfire that battle would be joined in the morning. The more experienced men fought the adrenalin and the anxiety, tried to settle the chatter of their younger comrades and find a few hours' rest. They too knew what day it was, the Nativity of St John, the voice crying in the wilderness, a man who would be persecuted and killed by an evil king, and they too ate frugally, as was fitting. Even those who had fought at Loudoun Hill, at Brander and other encounters, had been in the raiding parties and the retaking of the castles, knew that fear and the surges of adrenalin, what bards called 'battle frenzy' or 'the rage-fit', would carry them through.

Marshalling an army takes time, and according to one chronicler, it was not until a little before the third hour, or in modern reckoning around 8am to 9am, that the Scots emerged from the woods of the New Park to form up in battle order. Their schiltrons were all arrayed on the ground known as the dryfield of Balquhiderock. It lay between the Bannock Burn and the Pelstream Burn, what John Barbour described as a place of 'great straitness', meaning narrow. The land sloped down from the Park towards the carse, and it seems that the Scots chose to marshal a little way down the scarp. It may well have been in King Robert's mind that he needed to close with the English army as soon as he could in order to negate the withering fire of their archers. The armies were forming up close to each other and all that the Scots and their king did was observed.

When the ranks of the schiltrons formed, each man knew his place. In front and on the flanks stood the older and more experienced spearmen who knew what was to come. And who knew that at all costs the line must not be breached, that if a man fell, they must close up at once. Behind them, ready to project their spear-points between their comrades stood a second rank, and behind them a reserve, some of them probably shooters, men prepared to dash through the lines into the mêlée to kill or capture enemies who were in difficulties. Variations of these formations formed part of Scotland's history. Carved in the eighth century to depict the Battle of Dunnichen of 685, the Aberlemno Stone shows three ranks of Pictish spearmen with the second ranks pushing their weapons past the men in front of them.

Once the schiltrons had formed up, King Robert enacted two medieval military traditions. On the battlefield, in front of the whole army, he knighted Walter Stewart and conferred on James Douglas the dignity of knight banneret. His triangular pennon was replaced by a square standard, clear recognition of his renown and seniority. At the laying of the king's sword on their shoulders, the massed ranks of spearmen, especially Douglas and Stewart's schiltron, will have roared and cheered. The new knights' hearts will have leapt. And then, wheeling his warhorse to face his men, the king spoke.

In the midst of the army, protected by his priests and a hedge of spears, Abbot Bernard of Arbroath carried the Brecbennoch, the reliquary of St Columba. God's great saint of Scotland and all of his sacred power would fight that day with his faithful sons. Years later Bernard wrote down what he remembered of Bruce's speech before battle, perhaps with a little embellishment:

> My lords, my people, accustomed to enjoy that full freedom for which in times gone by the kings of Scotland have fought many a battle! For eight years or more I have struggled with much labour for my right to the kingdom and for honourable liberty. I have lost brothers, friends and kinsmen. Your own kinsmen have been made captive and bishops and priests are locked in prison. Our country's nobility has poured forth its blood in war. Those barons you can see before you, clad in mail, are bent on destroying me and oblit-

erating my kingdom, nay, our whole nation. They do not believe that we can survive. They glory in their warhorses and equipment. For us, the name of the Lord must be our hope of victory in battle.

This is a day of rejoicing: the birthday of John the Baptist. With our Lord Jesus as commander, Saint Andrew and the martyr Saint Thomas shall fight today with the saints of Scotland for the honour of their country and their nation. If you heartily repent of your sins you will be victorious, under God's command. As for offences committed against the Crown, I proclaim a pardon, by virtue of my royal power, to all those who fight manfully for the kingdom of our fathers.

After he had stirred their hearts, the king tried to settle their anxieties. All men who fell in battle would be excused any duties or payments that might be due on their deaths. Their families should not suffer loss twice. Having shown himself to his men in all the splendour of his royal war-gear, the man who had killed the charging de Bohun with only an axe, Bruce walked his horse back through the ranks towards the rear of the army.

Crows lifted off the trees of the New Park as trumpets sounded and banners were raised up for the march downhill to join battle. At their king's insistence, each schiltron unfurled the banners of their leaders and leading men. Above Edward Bruce's men flew the red chevron on a white ground of the earls of Carrick, the three white stars on an azure ground were for Douglas and the black birlinns of the Macdonald Lords of the Isles fluttered above the heads of their soldiers. And it was more than medieval show. Banners mattered in the ruck and confusion of battle as all inevitably became disordered when armies clashed and lines bulged, buckled or broke. The colours acted as rallying points where men could flock, find their comrades and re-form their ranks. But for now all was in order as the drummers beat a slow rhythm for the deliberate march of the schiltrons, their sergeants roaring to their men that they needed to keep their footing as the ranks moved over rough and tussocky ground, to move forward steadily in an unbroken line. With the drumbeat thud of the feet of thousands of men, the sound of impending battle rumbled down the dryfield towards the English army.

As knights were heaved into their saddles and formed up, the blazing colours of Engish chivalry lit the carse. But behind the finery lurked confusion. Where were the archers? The Scots appeared to be marching into range and even only a few companies of Edward II's longbowmen could have slowed the tramping resolve of the schiltrons to a more faltering, hesitant pace. And given how badly armoured knights had fared against the spear-hedges the day before, where were the English spearmen? It may be that tradition, orders of precedence with egos attached, were trumping any tactical common sense.

Bruce was attacking. In the past schiltrons had been static, defensive; Wallace's men had dug in at Falkirk, and at Courtrai the Flemings had stood behind ditches as the spearmen expected the charge of the armoured knights to bring the fight to them. But the king of Scots had set his men in echelon formation.

Edward Bruce led his schiltron on the right flank, keeping as close as possible to the declivity of the Bannock Burn on his right so that it could protect his flank. There were certainly detachments of English soldiers on the other side of the burn, the whole army had not crossed the night before. There were probably even archers, but they appeared to present no threat. With the banner of Carrick flying over them, Edward Bruce's brigade marched to the slow beat of drum a little ahead of the Earl of Moray's schiltron, and on his left was the brigade commanded by Sir James Douglas. King Robert kept his men in reserve, and the Islesmen of Aonghas Og Macdonald, with their Lochaber axes, will have wondered when and if their turn would come. It will have been difficult for the watchers in the English ranks to read, but the Scots were advancing in a stepped formation, the king's brother having the honour of leading the attack with Moray slightly behind and Douglas a few paces behind him. *Echelon* is a French word meaning the rungs or steps of a ladder, and the tactic was ancient, first used at the Battle of Leuctra in 371 BC when the Thebans defeated the hitherto invincible Spartans. Perhaps King Robert knew his history.

When the Scots army was still beyond the range of the English longbows – and some companies of archers appeared to be mustering in the English lines – a trumpet pierced the morning air and the echelons suddenly halted. Piety and good drill had persuaded the commanders that this planned pause was necessary. Beside a priest holding a crucifix aloft, the Abbot of Inchaffray stood forward from the ranks and signalled for the whole army to kneel in prayer. Across the battlefield, the English heard the low rumble of the Lord's Prayer, the Latin Paternoster, and moments before battle would surely be joined each soldier prayed to his God and asked forgiveness for his sins. The abbot held his right hand high, closed his eyes and called down God's benediction on the schiltrons.

By this time trumpets had sounded in the English army and

Edward II and his retinue were armoured and mounted. As he watched the Scots advance in open field, very clearly prepared to fight a pitched battle, to do what Bruce had avoided for eight years, the English king was astonished at a sight he had never thought to behold. 'What! Will those Scots fight?' And when the abbot made the sign of the cross and Bruce's army knelt to pray, Edward's astonishment and misreading of what he saw prompted, 'Those men kneel to ask for mercy.' In the royal retinue was the Scot, Sir Ingram de Umfraville, and it is said who he replied, 'You are right, they ask for mercy, but not from you. They ask it from God, for their sins.' Even bearing all the hallmarks of apocrypha – the sense that de Umfraville knew what was about to happen, the unlikely notion that an advancing army would suddenly kneel to beg mercy from an enemy – this exchange speaks to a sense of unwavering English self-confidence. The ragged, grey Scots might be advancing but as the squadrons of mounted knights in all their chivalric splendour formed up with their lords and the archers strung their bows, there could be no doubt that numbers would tell and the English army would simply rumble over these pious spear-carriers.

The Scots army probably halted to do more than pray. Having advanced over open but rough and hummocky ground, their decurions and commanders will have wanted to re-dress the ranks and straighten each of the three stepped lines. If the front ranks were not straight at the point of impact, even the slightest kink could offer an opening to charging horsemen or infantry. As the Scots shuffled back and forward, probably dressing to the right, as is still the habit on modern parade grounds, their commanders will have roared for their men to look to their fronts and when the time came to lower their long pikes, to hold them hard and steady for the crash of the charge. Discipline, iron discipline and gritted determination to fight in tight formation was what would defeat the prancing, snorting finery in front of them. Trumpets sounded once more, men exchanged glances, and the Scots began their slow march into history.

In 1298, William Wallace had deployed small companies of archers in his schiltrons at the Battle of Falkirk. Many were men from the Ettrick Forest, the vast tract of wild land to the west of Selkirk where Scottish kings had hunted game for almost two centuries. They carried short bows, perfect for stalking and shooting deer and other animals in rough and wooded terrain, but they were not war-bows and did have the range of the longbow. On a windless, fair day an Ettrick Forest archer could fly an arrow 200 yards or a little more. When the Scots bowmen loosed off the first volleys of the day at Bannockburn, the armies were clearly closing fast. Here is the account in the *Lanercost Chronicle*, almost certainly taken from an eyewitness:

> . . . when both sides had made themselves ready for battle, the English archers were thrown forward before the line, and the Scottish archers engaged them, a few being killed and wounded on either side; but the King of England's archers quickly put the others to flight.

Stung by this initial exchange, the Scottish commanders urged their men forward but roared for them to stay steady and keep in formation. By this stage, only 200 yards or less from the English lines, Edward Bruce and his front ranks could see that there was hesitation amongst the opposing cavalry. The temptation to surge forward must have been intense, but the Scots persisted with their deliberate pace, shoulder to shoulder, ready to lower the forest of pikes when the charge came.

At this pivotal point, Edward II appears to have lost control. Once again the earls of Gloucester and Hereford squabbled over who should have the honour of leading the knights of the vanguard into the first clash of battle. Hereford was Constable of England – he should lead! Gloucester's family, the de Clares, had a traditional right, had always been at the centre of the first charge. As these men argued, the drums of the Scots beat louder and the schiltrons drew closer.

Suddenly Gloucester snapped. Summoning companies of archers to support him with volleys, he mounted his destrier and from that vantage point could see that the enemy were closing fast. Without waiting for the archers or taking the time to put on his surcoat blazoned with the arms of his earldom, Gloucester shouted for the knights of the vanguard to form line, knee to knee, and they began to walk, trot, canter and quickly kick their destriers into the gallop. Thundering over the ground, covering the short distance between the armies in moments, they levelled their lances and roared their war-cries. Watching from the rear, Robert Bruce must have felt a mixture of relief and trepidation. Now that Gloucester and perhaps 500 knights were racing across the grass towards the waiting ranks of spearmen, the English archers could no longer send volleys into the sky for fear of friendly fire. But would his brother's line hold? Or would they crumple as the English smashed into them? The *Lanercost Chronicle*'s witness answered:

> When both armies engaged each other, and the great horses of the English charged the pikes of the Scots,

> as it were into a dense forest, there arose a great and terrible crash of spears broken and of destriers wounded to the death; and so they remained without movement for a while.

The charge had been a disaster. When the vanguard levelled their lances, the front rank of Edward Bruce's schiltron probably knelt down on one knee to butt their pikes into the ground and raised their points at an angle that might pierce the chest or the belly of a charging destrier. Its weight and momentum would do the rest if the pike did not snap. Their comrades having absorbed the shuddering shock of the charge, the second rank stood to jab their pikes at the mounted knights and perhaps, as at Falkirk, a third rank of bristling spear-points made a dense and fatal hedge. The English vanguard impaled itself on it.

As horses were stabbed and wounded, they went down squealing their death agonies, their metal-shod hooves thrashing wildly. Their riders were unhorsed, jabbed at by spearmen or perhaps killed by shooters who ran out from the ranks, their axes and dirks ready. Lances snapped and splintered as the fallers in the front rank of the English charge badly impeded those behind and momentum died. As the *Lanercost Chronicle* put it: 'They remained without movement for a while.' Unidentified, lacking his surcoat and its coat of arms, the Earl of Gloucester became isolated from his retinue, and in the ruck of the fighting, he was dragged off his destrier and hacked to death. Capture and a lucrative ransom would have been much preferable but the spearmen did not know who he was.

As dying horses thrashed their hooves, defecating involuntarily in their agonies, the stink of their muck and blood filling the morning air, the English knights tried again and again to push into the press of spearmen. It was as if no other tactic were possible. More famous names fell. The man who had led the attack on Moray's schiltron the night before, Sir Robert Clifford, was cut down. Elsewhere along the front of battle, Sir Pagan Tiptoft, Sir Edmund de Mauley, the Steward of Edward II's household, and Sir John Comyn, the Lord of Badenoch and son of the John Comyn killed by Bruce at the altar of the Greyfriars at Dumfries, were also pulled off their destriers and killed. John Barbour's description of all that ferocity was vivid:

> And Englishmen of great pride who were in their vanguard held their way straight to the division that Sir Edward [Bruce] commanded and led. They spurred their horses and galloped at them boldly, and [the Scots] met them hardily so that at their meeting there was such a smashing of spears that men could hear it far away. At their encounter, without doubt, many a steed was impaled, and many a good man borne down and killed: and many a valiant deed was done there bravely, for they assaulted each other stoutly with many [kinds of] weapons. Some of the horses that were stabbed reared and fell right roughly. But the rest, nonetheless, who could get to the encounter, did not hold back because of that hindrance, but attacked very strongly. And the Scots met them sturdily, with spears that were cutting-sharp, and axes that were well-ground, with which many a blow was struck. The fight there was so hard and fierce that many a worthy and brave man was felled in that struggle, and

> had no strength to rise again. The Scotsmen battled
> hard to overthrow their enemy's great power.

As the English vanguard engaged, it is likely that the schiltrons of the Earl of Moray and Sir James Douglas moved up to form a continuous line to avoid the danger of being flanked and to engage and press forward on the remainder of the English army. Between the Pelstream Burn and the Bannock Burn, the front was perhaps 1,000 yards long. Hand-to-hand fighting in such a murderous mêlée cannot have been continuous and as the charging knights drew back to re-form, the Scots will have caught their panting breath and tightened their ranks, plugging any gaps. Pauses will also have allowed the Scots to advance a few precious yards over the appalling debris of dead and dying horses, dead and dying men and compress the disorganised English ever more tightly. Bruce's plan was working. But for his enemy, something had to break the deadlock, and for Edward II, archers might turn the battle.

Companies were brought up through the congestion from the rear and they first attempted to fire volleys over the heads of their cavalry at the schiltrons, but only three or at most four ranks deep, they presented a very narrow target. Most English arrows fell behind the Scots. Tactics had to change. As the English line fragmented or drew back, and gaps appeared where horses and men lay dying, the archers attempted to fire at point-blank range, straight at the ranks of the Scots. But according to one chronicler, 'they hit few Scots in the breast but [were] striking more English in the back'.

It became quickly clear that a more open line of fire was essential and companies of English archers scrambled across the

Pelstream Burn to form up opposite the left flank of Sir James Douglas' schiltron. This time, it worked. Setting themselves six paces apart, the archers stabbed their sheaves of arrows into the ground and began loosing off volleys at the spearmen across the burn. Arrows began to find their marks in the close-packed ranks and as men fell and they thinned, Bruce acted. At his direction, Sir Robert Keith led a charge of 500 light horsemen, their spears levelled at the bowmen. And they scattered them. Such was the impetus of Keith's furious charge that it drove the fleeing archers back into their own ranks where their comrades were said to have attacked them.

But Douglas' schiltron had taken heavy casualties and the left flank of the 100-yard Scottish line was exposed. If the English army pushed hard on their right, they could break out and fatally flank Moray's and Edward Bruce's brigades. This was the moment of crisis. The king decided to commit his reserve schiltron, the men who had beaten back Gloucester and the vanguard the day before. The Islesmen raised the black birlinn banner of Clan Donald, Aonghas Og roared the war-cries of his ancestors and on either side of him the mail-clad gallowglasses advanced, their Lochaber axes glinting in the midsummer sun.

Bruce knew that he was now risking everything by sending the reserve brigade forward. Nothing now could prevent the English from forcing their way across the Pelstream or Bannock burn and attacking the Scots line from the rear. All they lacked was generalship. 'My hope is constant in thee,' said the king to Aonghas Og and his chiefs.

As they advanced to the front, many of the Islesmen and the Highlanders will have begun to murmur the names of the army of the dead, summoning them to come to the field and fight beside them. In the moments before battle was joined, the Gaelic-speaking warriors recited the *sloinneadh*, the naming of the names of their lineages, the names of revered memory. 'Is mise mac Iain, mac Domhnaill, mac Ruaridh, I am the son of John, the son of Donald, the son of Rory.' Many could murmur back through the glories of their ancient genealogies for more than 20 generations and they summoned the ghosts of an immense past to march beside them. As they moved forward in close formation, the mail-clad gallowglasses, the feared heavy Highland infantry presented a new threat to the milling ranks of English cavalry, men-at-arms and spearmen. A fifteenth-century commentator wrote 'these sort of men be those that do not lightly abandon the field, but bide the brunt to the death'. Many were minor aristocrats able to afford the long coat of ring-mail that reached to their knees, and the double-bladed Lochaber axe. These metal coats were sometimes known as jacks and to protect their legs, the gallowglasses wore jackboots.

Now the battle raged, eddied and boiled as men pushed and hacked at those before them. Bruce used his brigade to reinforce, to bolster tired men, take the places of the wounded or the exhausted, their spears like lead in their hands, their muscles aching. Pushing hard along the whole front, the Scots began to advance yard by yard, compressing the English army into an ever-shrinking pocket between the two burns, forcing them backwards into the carse where their camp had been, where pools and sikes waited. Bruce's fresh brigade fought fiercely, giving new impetus. Here is Barbour's breathless verse:

> ... with all their might and main they laid into [them]
> like men out of their wits. Where they could strike
> with a full stroke, there no armour could withstand

> their blow. They cut down those they could overtake, and gave such blows with axes that they split heads and helmets. Their foes met them right boldly and laid into them doughtily with weapons that were of strong steel. The battle was well fought there. There was such a din of blows, as weapons landing on armour, such a great breaking of spears, such pressure and such pushing, such snarling and groaning.

Swinging their Lochaber axes at the legs of the destriers to hamstring them, the gallowglasses and the other Highlanders began to bring down knights. The English were now packed so tight that even if a man slipped and fell, he was lost, trampled underfoot by his comrades or the hooves of skittering horses. Like a seismic shudder, something born of 100 incidents, a sense of defeat rippled through the English ranks. Knights threw down their swords and maces, held up their hands to yield, spearmen gave ground and in the disordered mêlée archers knew that their deadly skill meant nothing. Suddenly a roar resonated along the front of the schiltrons. 'On them! On them! They fail!' The cry ricocheted and the English heard it too as the Scots pushed harder and harder.

And English hearts sank even lower when they saw what must have appeared as a fresh Scots army rush out of the trees of the New Park. Banners flew over a dense, charging mass of men who roared 'Slay, slay on them hastily!' as they raced down the slope towards the front, their weapons raised. This was not the steady advance of the schiltron but the headlong attack of those who knew that victory was coming. In fact it was no army but a muster of those known as 'the small folk', servants and labourers who had been left in the Park to guard the baggage and supplies. They too sniffed victory and streamed across the battlefield, across the blood-soaked grass, through the stink and mess of dead men and horses, to join the fighting and perhaps join in the plunder that would follow. Their arrival on the field cannot have pleased Bruce. His chosen men were doing their part, and the small folk were not needed. If victory was indeed close, let there not be carnage but capture. Ransoms would be useful after all the costs of war, and the king's chivalric instincts were repelled by needless butchery. But all was not won yet.

Edward II was still fighting, and had fought hard and courageously in the thick of battle. He had one destrier badly piked under him and when Scots had taken hold of his horse's caparison, the English king beat them off with his mace. The royal retinue had come under savage attack and the shieldbearer, Sir Roger Northburgh, was pulled down and captured. This was all becoming too dangerous, the brunt of battle too close. Aymer de Valence and Sir Giles d'Argentan defended Edward, but they quickly began to realise that not only did defeat stare them squarely in the face, the Scots were so close that they might kill, or even worse, capture the king. That would have been utterly calamitous and the two men pulled at the reins of the royal destrier to take him, protesting and resisting, out of the ruck of the fighting. And that signalled the moment of victory for Bruce. When the English soldiers saw the royal standards leave the field, their ranks broke and defeat turned into a rout. But not along the entire 100-yard front.

There was still resistance on the right flank, where Edward Bruce's schiltron had fought bravely throughout the long morning. When de Valence and Sir Giles d'Argentan had mustered a protective force of about 500 knights around their fleeing king, the great knight of Christendom could not flee with them. His honour would not allow it and d'Argentan said to his king:

> Sire, your rein was committed to me; you are now in safety; there is your castle where your person may be safe. I am not accustomed to fly, nor am I going to begin now. I commend you to God.

He rode back to the front, plunged into the fighting with Bruce's spearmen and was cut to pieces. He could not live with the disgrace of what had happened on the banks of the Bannock Burn and impaled himself on Scottish spears.

Within only a few minutes of leaving the field, the English king and his knights clattered up the steep hill to seek sanctuary at the gates of Stirling Castle. But there was none. Sir Philip Moubray had the drawbridge raised, explaining to Edward II that if he allowed him inside, he would surely become a captive. And the arrival of the king and so many knights telling him all he needed to know about what had happened at Bannockburn, the governor was no doubt thinking of his own future. The English king wheeled his fresh horse and with his retinue around him, rode to the west of the New Park, around the rear of the Scottish army, and made for the Tor Wood and the Roman road. Pursued by Sir James Douglas, who had only 60 or so horsemen at his back, Edward and his party 'had not the leisure to make water' before they reached the safety of Dunbar Castle. Still loyal to the English cause, Earl Patrick saw his defeated lord onto a ship bound for Bamburgh. Hugh Despenser was also on board, without his furniture.

Meanwhile the rout at Bannockburn was claiming many lives. As they stampeded into the ditch of the burn, or ran north to the Forth, pushed by the panic behind them, many men and horses drowned. Barbour wrote these memorable lines:

> When Sir Aymer had fled with the king, there was none who dared remain, but [all] fled scattering in every direction, their foes pressing them hard. Truth to tell, they were so terrified, and they fled in fear so fast, that a very great part of them fled to the River Forth and there most of them were drowned; Bannock Burn between [its] banks was so filled with men and horse that men could pass dry-foot over it on drowned horses and men. Lads, boys and rabble, when they saw the [English] force defeated, ran among them and killed them like men who could put up no defence – it was dreadful to see.

The Earl of Hereford rode south-west for Bothwell Castle in the Clyde Valley. It was still nominally in English hands and Walter Gilbertson opened the gates to the earl and several other lords. And promptly made them prisoner. In October 1314, King Robert exchanged these men for his queen, Elizabeth, his daughter, Marjorie, his sister, Mary, who had been so cruelly confined in a cage, and old Robert Wishart, the Bishop of Glasgow who had given Bruce such splendid vestments and a banner for his coronation. Blind and having suffered much, the old man must have rejoiced in victory as much as release.

In the aftermath of battle, King Robert was magnanimous and thoughtful. Raoul de Monthermer had been Earl of Gloucester before Gilbert de Clare and had famously warned Bruce of his impending arrest in 1305/06. Made captive at Bannockburn, he was returned to his family without ransom. The body of young Gloucester was also sent to his family without conditions. But there was one English prisoner who was forced to make amends. A Carmelite friar, Robert Baston, accompanied Edward II's army as its bard, his pen poised to write a paean of victory. He was promised release on condition that he first composed a poem to celebrate the English defeat. In a typically playful translation from the original Latin, Edwin Morgan rendered the last two stanzas in this way:

> What is truth worth? How can I sing about so much
> blood?
> Could even tragedy bare its breast to show such cut
> and thud?
> The names may be famous but I do not know
> them all.
> I cannot number the humblings and tumblings of
> hundreds that fall.
> Many are mown down, many are thrown down,
> Many are drowned, many are found and bound.
> Many are taken in chains for a stated ransom.
> So some are rising, riding rich high and handsome
> Who were before the war poor and threadbare souls.
> The battlefield is barren but piled with spoils.
> Shouts and taunts and vengeful cuts and brawls –
> I saw, but what can I say? A harvest I did not sow!
> Guile is not my style. Justice and peace are what
> I would show.

Anyone who has more in store, let him write the score.
My mind is numb, my voice half-dumb, my art a blur.

I am a Carmelite, and my surname is Baston.
I grieve that I survive a happening so harrowing and
    ghastly.
If it is my sin to have left out what should be in,
Let others begin to record it, without rumour or spin.

7
A Kingdom Won

'How can I sing of so much blood?'

The killing did not stop. More men may have died in flight than in the fighting. As panic drove the English into the ditches of the Bannock Burn, the Pelstream Burn, into the pows and sikes of the carse and into the sucking mud and tides of the River Forth, many drowned or were trampled, their heads forced down into asphyxiation, their bodies pinned by the press of men and horses who had fallen on top of them. And these thousands of deaths in the mud and bitter saltwater will not have been silent. As their ribcages snapped, crushed in the rack of bodies, men screamed in agony, implored their God to take them, begged for mercy. But there was none.

Those disciplined spearmen of the Scottish schiltrons, suddenly released, pursued their enemies in all directions, thirsting for blood, after all the pushing and hacking and stabbing of the battle front, suddenly running, adrenalin surging, after the panicking English soldiers, running them down like hounds after foxes. And when they brought them down, death might have been quicker than for those whose lives gasped out of them on the bed of the Bannock Burn. As the Lanercost chronicler wrote, 'Horsemen and foot alike, noblemen, knights and squires, archers and infantry, were seized with the need to escape.' Some who were caught by groups of spearmen were disarmed, hamstrung by cuts behind their knees so that they collapsed, immobile, utterly defenceless when the plunderers returned. Others reckoned to be valuable for ransom were rounded up as prisoners, bound and probably relieved of anything valuable, including boots and clothing. Some will have shivered in their sarks, their hands and feet tied, humiliated, lying in the mosses, waiting to be taken by whichever lord or band had captured them.

Blows from bladed weapons rarely kill outright and many men will have lain on the field, their bodies lacerated and broken, but they were not yet dead. As Barbour recorded, the Small Folk went about the battlefield dispatching and robbing these wounded men, a sight that 'was dreadful to see'. Over a wide area, where the flight of the English had taken them beyond the narrow place where the battle had been fought between the two burns, the corpses of horses and men lay in the late afternoon of midsummer's day, 1314, clouds of flies buzzed, feasting on the blood and guts and involuntary defecation that was the deposit of a great victory. As the sun climbed high in the summer sky and the din and chaos of battle stilled, the grisly price of glory was revealed.

In places there was organised resistance. Led by Sir Maurice Berkeley and perhaps by Aymer de Valence, a large company of Welsh infantry either fought their way off the battlefield, or were simply ignored in favour of easier pickings. Several thousand strong, they beat a fighting retreat over the hill trails of the Southern Uplands to the shores of the Solway Firth. Attacked and harried by Scottish skirmishers, they survived to wade across to Burgh by Sands and gain sanctuary at Carlisle. One of the earliest reports of the rout at Bannockburn appeared in the chronicle of the Welsh monastery of Valle Crucis and it may have been given by one of what Lanercost called 'the fugitive Welsh'.

On the battlefield knights surrendered and one, Sir Marmaduke Thweng, was a veteran of the English expeditions to Scotland. After having spent the night after the battle in hiding (in a bush, it was said), he laid down his weapons in front of King Robert and was not only permitted to return home to Kilton Castle in Yorkshire without the need to pay ransom but also given gifts. Many English footsoldiers had fled towards Stirling Castle, and, refused admission, had mustered in bands below the rock. They could have been dangerous but they began to surrender in large numbers.

When the plundering was exhausted, the grim business of burial began. Barbour recounted how noblemen were interred in the holy ground around churches while mass graves were dug for the infantry and archers who had died on the battlefield. Many small groups of men will have escaped into the Tor Wood and at first light on the day after midsummer will have begun the long and dangerous walk home to England.

The day after the battle Sir Philip Moubray opened the gates of Stirling Castle and in the elegant contemporary phrase, 'came into King Robert's peace'. At the same time, Patrick, Earl of Dunbar, surrendered and both men swore allegiance. The sole Scottish town and castle remaining in English hands was Berwick, and for three weeks after Bannockburn, King Edward set up headquarters there as remnants of his defeated army converged. Having ridden north from Bamburgh, he met those escorting knights and others who had come south from Dunbar. Recriminations probably echoed around Berwick's great hall. Ever chivalrous and generous in victory, Bruce sent the bodies of the Earl of Gloucester and Sir Robert Clifford to Berwick so that they could be taken on to their families. Gloucester was King

Robert's brother-in-law and on the night after the battle, when most men would be celebrating, he kept a knightly vigil with the earl's corpse.

Bannockburn had been unusually bloody. Protected by their mail and armour, used to sweeping all before them in the charge, and open to ransom if captured, relatively few mounted knights died in war. Bannockburn was different. In the grim, compressed ruck of the fighting between the two burns Barbour reckoned that many knights were killed and more trampled to death in the rout. 'Two hundred pairs of red spurs were taken from dead knights.' More conservative estimates count 150 or so killed or captured, while on the Scottish side, Sir William Airth was cut down at Cambuskenneth and only William Vipoint and Walter Ross died on the battlefield. When the English king's standards were seen fleeing and Edward's army turned and ran, the casualty list will have lengthened.

King Robert also had Edward II's royal shield and his privy seal sent to Berwick. These were prestigious prizes, but not of much intrinsic value. The plunder picked up on the field was, however, of immense value and when added to the cash raised by ransoms, it made a significant economic impact on Scotland, a nation repeatedly ravaged by war. Bannockburn was a signal triumph and the Lanercost chronicler summed up its effect:

> After the aforesaid victory Robert de Brus was commonly called King of Scotland by all men, because he had acquired Scotland by force of arms.

But the battle did not end the war for Scotland.

Between the English and Scottish kings there followed a

long stand-off after Bannockburn. Bruce had established himself in Scotland and was internationally recognised as rightful king. But the threat from the south remained. Defending Scotland 'with a long stick', the king began to organise a series of devastating raids into northern England. In 1314 Edward Bruce led an expedition that reached as far south as Richmond before returning to Scotland through Cumbria and the Eden Valley, Carlisle and Liddesdale. Raids were not always successful. Based on an important Roman fortress of the first century AD, Carlisle Castle is not impressive but it is difficult to take. The town was also surrounded by high medieval walls and when King Robert trundled his siege engines against them in the summer of 1315, they could make little impression. A spirited defence led by Sir Andrew de Harcla was one deterrent, but the other was the weather. In the summer of 1315 it began to rain – almost incessantly. The climate was changing as northern Europe entered the long sequence of periods of bad weather known as the Little Ice Age. So much rain fell in the summer of 1315 that not only did Bruce's siege engines founder and topple in the mud, crops also failed, blackened by the damp and cold. Famine followed in 1316, and the Scottish raids in the north were particularly punitive.

If King Robert had won his kingdom by force of arms and acted aggressively to defend it, he was also determined to act emphatically in shaping the peace. A stream of legal and diplomatic documents were issued from the 'king's chapel' or chancery at Arbroath Abbey. Run by Abbot Bernard, the chancellor, this secretariat was much concerned with the attitude of the papacy towards Scotland's independence and the Scottish Church. The fourteenth century saw a long-lasting papal schism and both England and Scotland recognised the pope in Avignon. John

XXII had vigorously disciplined Church leaders for refusing to accept his English nominees for Scottish sees. Not only were four leading bishops excommunicated, but the pope had also cast King Robert out of the Church. This circumstance presented all sorts of difficulties and urgently required resolution.

In March 1320 the royal council met near Edinburgh at Newbattle Abbey to agree a policy towards the papacy. This was communicated to John XXII and his curia in the form of three letters; one from King Robert, a second from Bishop Lamberton of St Andrews and a third which became very famous. Sent by the earls, the barons and the freeholders on behalf of the Community of the Realm of Scotland, this letter to the pope has become known as the Declaration of Arbroath. What this remarkable document expressed was nothing less than a new sense of nationhood, a sense that Scotland was different and even unique, and a sense that the Community of the Realm could influence profoundly the actions and status of the king. In many important ways, the Declaration of Arbroath was the most enduring legacy of all the blood spilt at Bannockburn.

Written in superb medieval Latin, wasting barely a word, quite unlike the usual output of a fourteenth-century chancery, the Declaration is a masterpiece of precision. The author may indeed have been Abbot Bernard, but whoever composed what appears to be the work of one hand and mind, they understood how to use history to inform and underwrite the politics of the present. All nations needed an origin legend, a myth-historical story that reaches back into the darkness of the past and from the first marks out that nation as different. If it was his choice, then Abbot Bernard chose wisely as he based the origins of the Scots on a migration through the Mediterranean by way of Iberia.

Trojans, Scythians and warlike barbarians all appear, but the tale woven may not be so fanciful. Recent ancestral DNA research supports the supposedly fantastical opening of the Declaration, suggesting that many early settlers came to what is now Scotland in the millennia after the end of the last Ice Age – from the Iberian peninsula.

But when Bernard came to deal with the most difficult problem of the politics of the present, he showed a mastery of classical sources. Lifting material from biblical texts, especially the apocryphal Book of Maccabees, an account of a Jewish rebellion against Rome, and conflating it with the story of the Catiline Conspiracy written by the historian Sallust, he eloquently navigated his way around the central problem that the Community of the Realm had in reality overthrown the rightful king, John Balliol, and replaced him with Robert Bruce. In order to avoid the charge of illegitimacy, the Declaration had to enshrine the possibility that Robert or a succeeding king of Scotland could also be rejected by the Community of the Realm and replaced. Here is a translation of the key passage, surely one of the most persuasive, elegant and inspirational political statements made in medieval Europe:

> But from these countless evils we have been set free, by the help of him who though he afflicts yet heals and restores, by our most tireless prince, king and lord, the lord Robert. He, that his people might be delivered out of the hands of our enemies, met toil and fatigue, hunger and peril, like another Maccabaeus or Joshua, and bore them cheerfully. Him, too, divine providence, his right of succession according to our laws

> and customs which we shall maintain to the death, and due consent and assent of us all, have made our prince and king. To him, as the man by whom salvation has been wrought unto our people, we are bound both by law and by his merits that our freedom may still be maintained, and by him, come what may, we mean to stand.
>
> Yet if he should give up what he has begun, and agrees to make us and our kingdom subject to the king of England or the English, we should exert ourselves at once to drive him out as our enemy and a subverter of his own rights and ours, and make some other man, who was well able to defend us, our king; for, as long as but a hundred of us remain alive, never will we on any conditions be brought under English rule. It is in truth not for glory, nor riches, nor honours that we are fighting, but for freedom – for that alone, which no honest man gives up but with life itself.

What this extraordinary passage illustrates is a political journey, one made by the Community of the Realm of Scotland, one of the poorest nations of medieval Europe, a journey from the support of an absolute monarchy to one that had been qualified after 30 years of war, upheaval and repeated threats of extinction.

Eight years after Bannockburn those threats remained very real. In 1322 Edward II once more mustered an expedition to conquer Scotland, his ambition to avenge 1314 undimmed. But this time there was to be no pitched battle. Bruce retreated, again scorching the earth in front of the English advance and although Edward's army reached Edinburgh, the lack of provision forced them eventually to turn back south. Five years later, the English king's long battle with his barons culminated in his deposition and then his murder at Berkeley Castle. Some chroniclers reported that he had been strangled or suffocated, others that he died in unspeakable agony as a red-hot iron was shoved into his anus. A year later, Bruce's war with England came to a formal end as commissioners for the young Edward III negotiated the Treaty of Edinburgh. It was to prove only a temporary respite.

In the latter part of his reign, King Robert preferred to spend his days at his house at Cardross on the Firth of Clyde. A Gaelic-speaking part of his realm, on the western sea roads, he must have felt comfortable there. Chroniclers wrote of Bruce's last illness as 'la grosse maladie', and Sir Thomas Grey recorded that he suffered from leprosy. This last observation may have been coloured by antipathy, and in any case it seems unlikely. Lepers were usually kept apart for fear of contagion, but when his condition allowed it, the king took a full part in government, meeting councillors, friends and diplomats. One chronicler believed that the king's illness came from 'cold lying' in the hills and wild places when Bruce fought guerrilla campaigns after 1306.

When the end came on 7 June 1329, almost exactly 15 years after Bannockburn, the king asked that his heart should be removed, embalmed and taken to the Holy Sepulchre in Jerusalem by a knight who would fight the infidels. Bruce had always wanted to go on crusade and if his mortal body could not see the holy city, then his heart might go there.

In 1330 Sir James Douglas sailed from Montrose harbour with 'many knights' and his king's embalmed heart safe in a casket. They joined the army of King Alfonso XI of Castile and Leon in the wars of reconquest of Muslim Spain. At a battle at

Teba de Ardales, north of Malaga, Douglas and his comrades were surrounded by Moorish cavalry and Bruce's great commander died as he tried to cut his way out. The king's heart was retrieved, brought back to Scotland and buried at Melrose Abbey. Two years later, Thomas Randolph, Earl of Moray and Sir Robert Keith were both dead. The band of brothers who had met in the woods of the New Park on the night of 23 June 1314 and decided to fight a battle for a nation were now all gone.

8

A Battle Lost

'They spurred their horses and galloped at them boldly, and [the Scots] met them hardily so that at their meeting there was such a smashing of spears that men could hear it far away.' 'The Bruce', John Barbour

Stern, heavily armoured, resolute and regal, the skirts of the destrier's caparison hinting at movement, King Robert's bronze statue sits high over the scene of his great triumph. Close at hand stands a rotunda, a more abstract monument to martial glory, and to give information there is a visitor centre run by the National Trust for Scotland. Nearby was the Borestone, traditionally where Bruce planted the royal standard on the morning of the second day of the battle. It was the very first memorial at Bannockburn, a flat stone about 3 feet in diameter and 2 feet thick with a circular hole or socket where a flagpole might have been set. Visited by the curious since the eighteenth century, one them Robert Burns, the Borestone grew ever smaller as souvenir fragments were chipped off. The last two bits were finally placed in the visitor centre.

Since the late nineteenth century, debate has swirled around the precise site of the second, decisive day of the battle. Five different locations have been vigorously argued, with some of the more perceptive comments coming from retired soldiers, and a consensus now believes that the schiltrons marched in echelon on dry ground between the Pelstream Burn to the north-west and the Bannock Burn to the south-east. Practicality prompts a little more precision. As the ground falls towards the carse and the flat, boggy ground by the Forth, there is a steep bank, too steep for heavily armoured cavalry to charge up it. Therefore it is thought likely that the Earl of Gloucester led his knights into the gallop across the flatter, dry ground a little further to the east. But no one is sure.

Two difficulties cloud a clear picture of precisely where history was made on 24 June 1314. The terrain is much changed from the days when Bruce and his famous captains rode around it, choosing their ground, planning how they might manoeuvre Edward II's unwieldy, squabbling army into a position that would compress and weaken it. Knowing that they could not fight all of the English and win, they had to find a means of using the landscape to break up a force at least twice as large. But it is now difficult to see it how they saw it. Modern drainage schemes have converted the woodland, the tussocky pasture, and the wet and boggy carseland into flat, tidy and fertile fields. While the gorge of the Bannock Burn remains an obstacle, the Pelstream Burn is much diminished, its banks now presenting no barrier. By the middle of the eighteenth century, the woods of the New Park had been cut down and much of its site has now disappeared under nineteenth- and twentieth-century housing while roads criss-cross the area, the hum of the M9 only a few hundred yards from Bruce's statue.

Battlefields are silent places, the war-cries, trumpets, drums and screams of conflict long stilled, but archaeologists have sometimes found them eloquent. Even in acidic soil metal arrowheads can be picked up, often on the surface, turned up by deep ploughing or discovered by the buzz of a metal detector. Many sheaves of arrows flew into the air above Bannockburn but little or no trace of them has yet been found. Many men died as the schiltrons and heavy cavalry clashed but none of the mass graves described by Barbour have turned up. In 2001 a series of exploratory excavations by Tony Pollard and Neil Oliver failed to find any trace of pits, skeletal remains, or indeed any other evidence that a great battle had been fought across that landscape. Finds of the pits or pots and their stakes at the Entry were reported in the late nineteenth century and the early twentieth but were not properly recorded. And that is all.

It appears that Bannockburn has disappeared. The epoch-making triumph won by Bruce and his chosen men has been lost. And this is more than a curious quirk of history; it leaves a substantial gap in understanding and appreciating the brilliance of King Robert and his commanders as tacticians. Their defeat of the English depended on their use of the ground as they would attempt to move Edward and his army around it. First blocking them and their use of the Roman road at the Entry, then forcing the long line of infantry, cavalry and supply wagons off the metalled surface, pushing them east to where the Bannock Burn was less steep-sided and could be crossed by large numbers, and then confining them overnight in the unsuitable carseland before advancing in echelon to a point where the Scottish battle-front trapped the milling cavalry, infantry and archers in a shrinking triangular pocket between the two burns. As Bruce, Douglas, Moray, Edward Bruce, Aonghas Og Macdonald and Keith discussed all of this, they knew that in battle anything could happen and often did. But this might just work. And it did. Spectacularly.

For a nation that appears to be endlessly fascinated by shifting notions of nationhood, Scotland is unusual in that it has no national anthem, nothing to stir the soul in the way that 'Land of My Fathers' does for all Welshmen and -women. The closest we have is the dirge-like 'Flower of Scotland' and of course its emotional tug comes racing across the centuries from Bannockburn, from the unlikely victory of a small nation that faced the army of a large one. Leaving aside ambivalence over the sentiments, it is surely a powerful testimony to the memory of Bruce's immense achievement that rugby stadia reverberate with a song based on the deeds of the chosen men and their captains.

Unlike Flodden or Culloden, both still open farmland and moorland, Bannockburn has changed a great deal over seven centuries as history has tramped again and again over the ground. But the memory of what happened on midsummer's day in 1314 is surely undimmed by gaps in knowledge. Enough is known to understand the tremendous significance of what took place. It was a battle that won a nation, a kingdom for a new king, the greatest warrior ever to wear the crown of Scotland. To stand at the foot of his statue and look up at Bruce's stern gaze is to look at a man whose raw courage and intelligence helped shape Scotland. And to look around at the modern landscape, the housing and the motorways is not to break a spell or be distracted. To adapt a Gaelic phrase, at Bannockburn it is still possible to hear the music of the thing as it happened.

Bibliography

Sometimes what appears to us in retrospect to be important, even epoch-changing, is little recorded by contemporaries. It was just news, what was happening, not necessarily history in the making. But Bannockburn was different and its significance was well understood at the time. Consequently there are several good sources and most of them broadly agree. And most of those close to the events of 1314 are English – for once, an example of the losers writing history. The relevant passages of the *Lanercost Chronicle* (written at Lanercost Priory, not far from Carlisle) and Sir Thomas Grey's *Scalachronica* (composed in north Northumberland) were almost certainly related by eyewitnesses, English soldiers who had escaped the slaughter and survived the rout. And both are easily accessible online. *The Life of Edward II* was the work of the Monk of Malmesbury and it also supplies useful information. For a Scottish perspective, the excellent series of selections from the version of the *Scotichronicon* by Walter Bower edited by D.E.R. Watt is very helpful, but the most fulsome account of the battle is in John Barbour's great epic, 'The Bruce'. Written in 1375, it relied for the details of Bannockburn and of King Robert's life again on those who had been involved. Allowing for literary flourish and the occasional wild exaggerations, particularly in the numbers fighting on each side, the poem is an extremely valuable resource, full of colour and insight. The edition and translation by A.A.M. Duncan is magisterial and thoroughly to be recommended.

A brief list of recommended secondary sources follows, but one must be singled out. First published almost 50 years ago, in 1965, and updated in 1988, G.W.S. Barrow's *Robert Bruce and the Community of the Realm of Scotland* is simply great history writing, a treatment of the king and his times unlikely ever to be surpassed. Barrow is a great scholar and his life of Bruce is his greatest work.

Armstrong, Pete, *Bannockburn 1314*, Osprey, 2002.

Barrow, G.W.S., *Robert Bruce and the Community of the Realm of Scotland*, Edinburgh University Press, 1965.

Brown, Chris, *Bannockburn 1314: A New History*, The History Press, 2013.

Caldwell, David H., *Scotland's Wars and Warriors*, The Stationery Office (formerly HMSO), 1998.

Gravett, Christopher, *English Medieval Knight, 1308–1400*, Osprey, 2002.

Hardy, Robert, *Longbow: A Social and Military History*, J.H. Haynes, 1976.

Lynch, Michael, *Scotland: A New History*, Century, 1991.

McDonald, R. Andrew, *The Kingdom of the Isles*, Tuckwell Press, 1997.

McNamee, Colm, *The Wars of the Bruces*, Tuckwell Press, 1997.

Moffat, Alistair, *The Borders,* Birlinn, 2007.

Morris, Marc, *A Great and Terrible King: Edward I and the Forging of Britain*, Hutchinson, 2008.

Reese, Peter, *Bannockburn*, Canongate, 2000.

Sadler, John, *Border Fury: England and Scotland at War 1296–1568*, Pearson, 2005.

Appendix 1
Maps

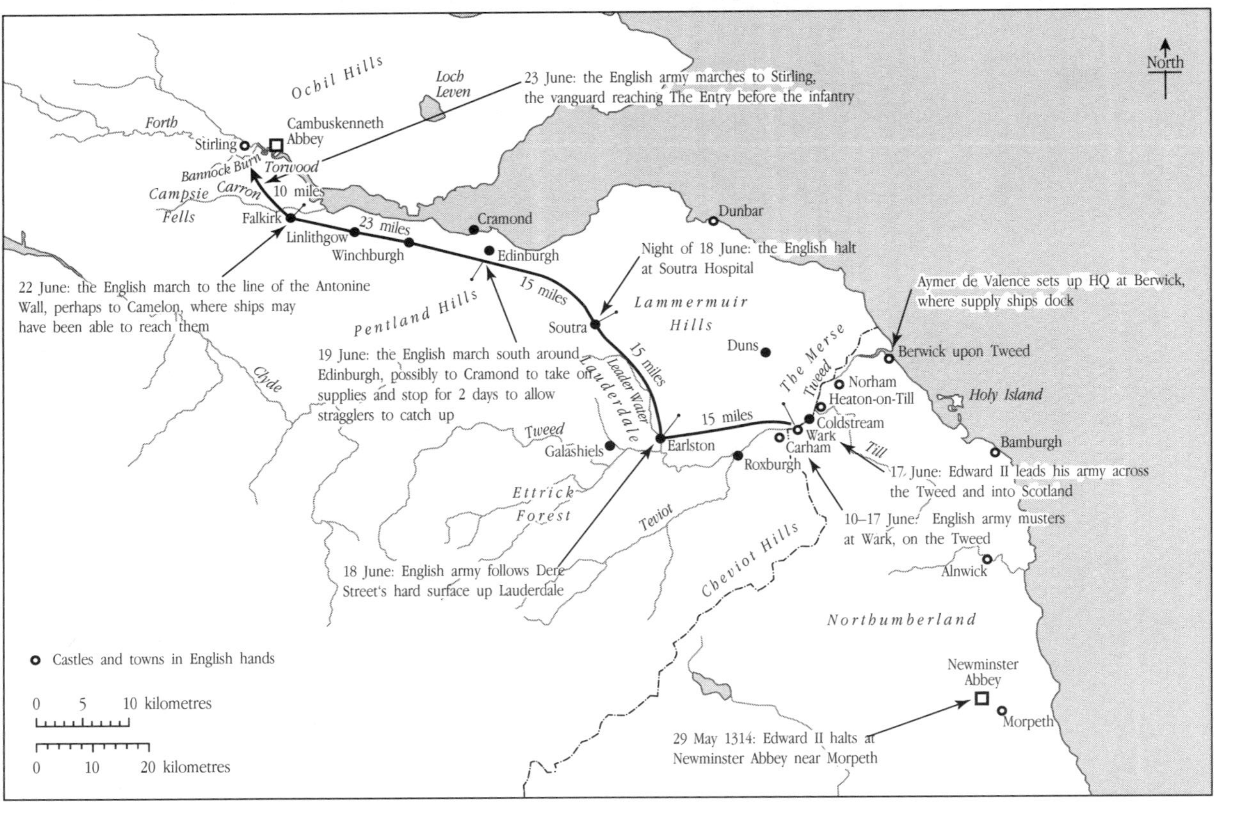

The Journey North

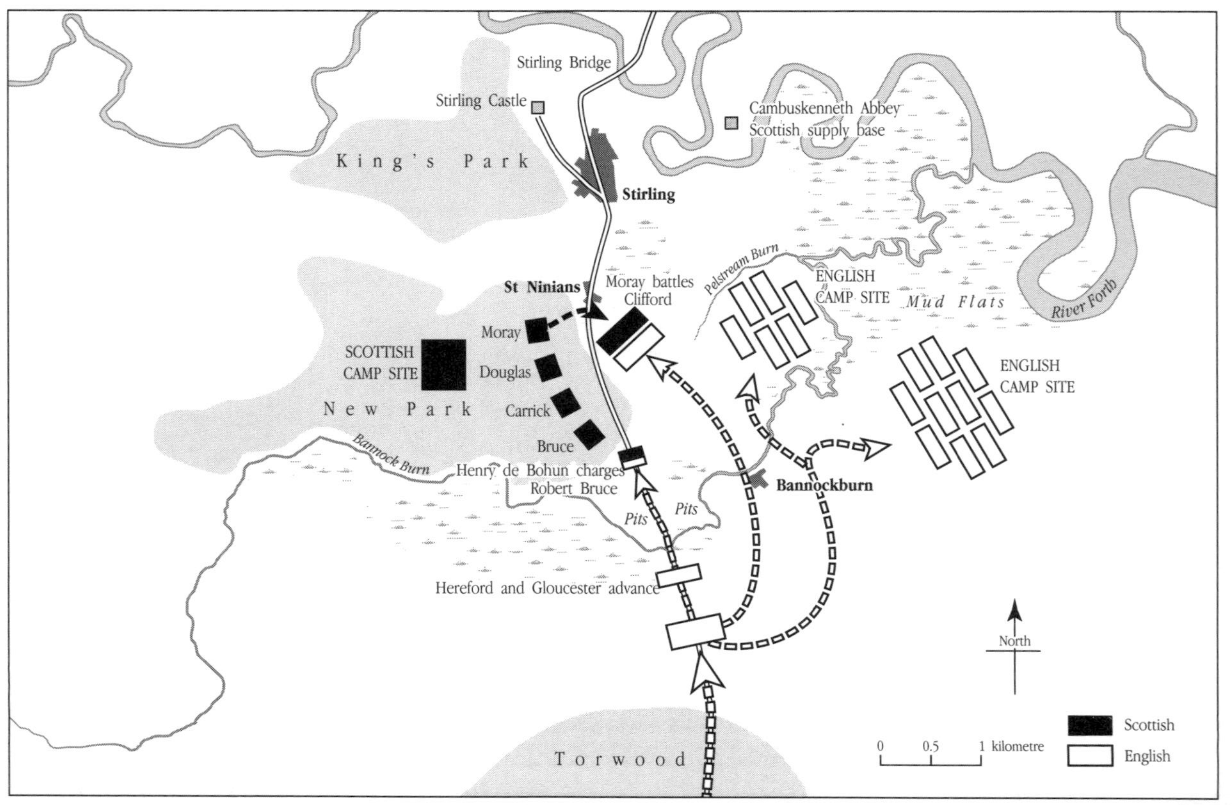

Bloody Sunday, 23 June 1314

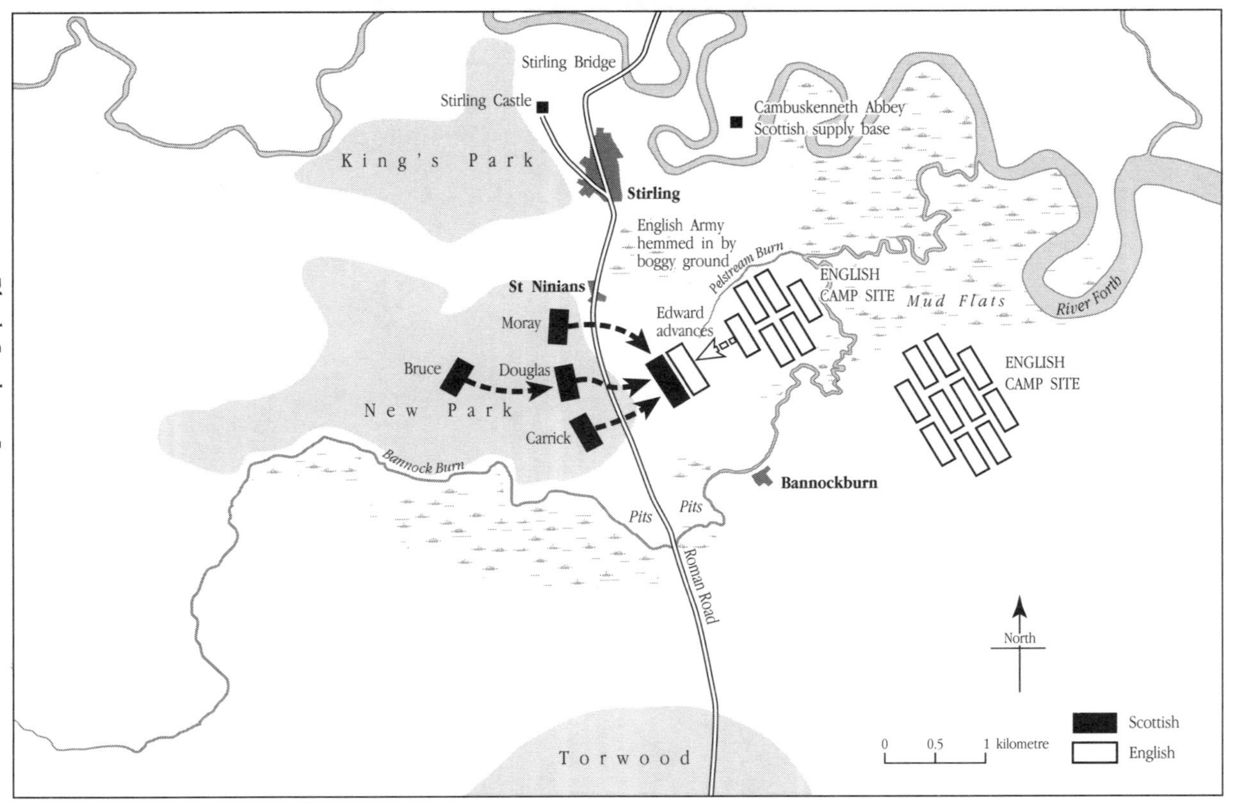

Bloody Sunday, 23 June 1314

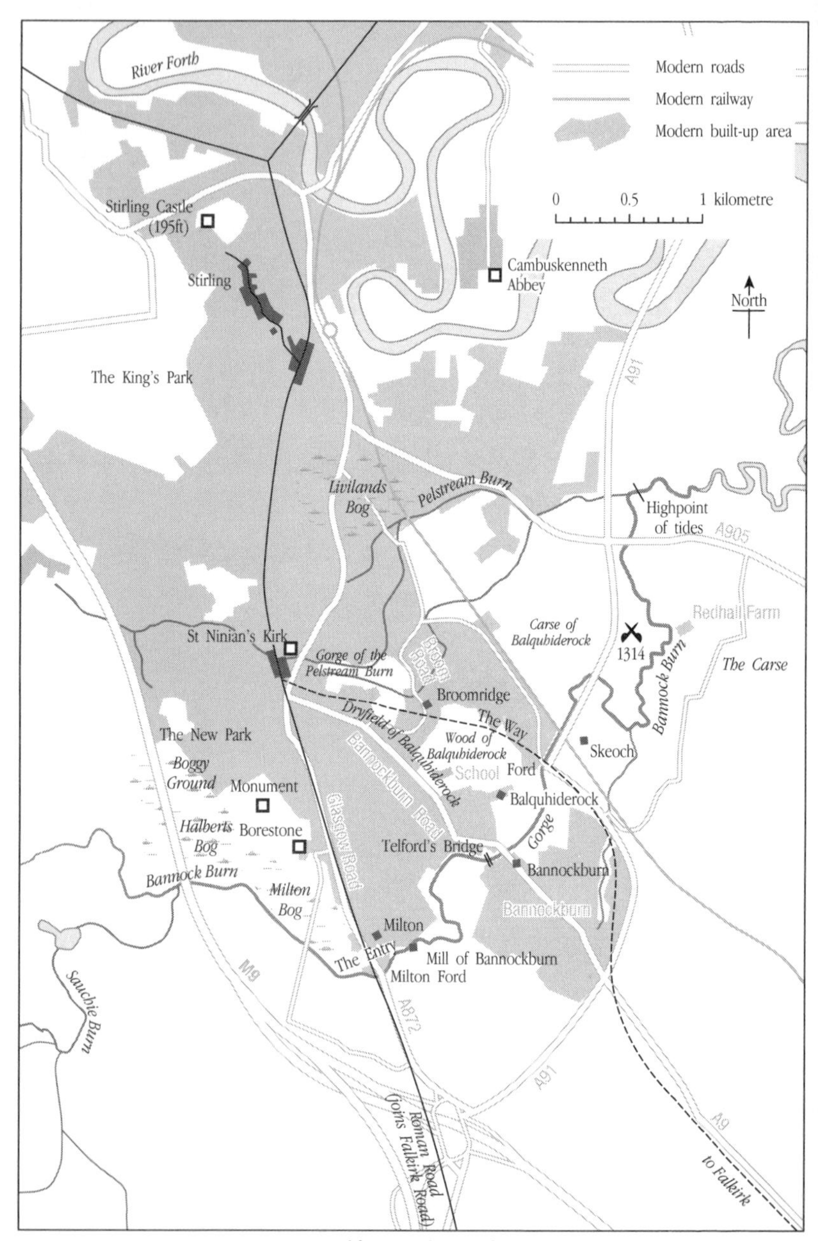

Bannockburn – then and now

Appendix 2
Dramatis Personæ

What follows is a series of brief biographical sketches of those involved in the battle at Bannockburn and those immediately affected by its outcome, notes which sometimes say a little more than the pace of the main narrative allowed. The most obvious way of arranging this would have been to list these men and women in battle order, the English on one side and the Scots on the other. But Bannockburn was not fought on simple national lines. Several Scots fought for Edward II and in any case the national distinction is not always apt. Between the Pelstream Burn and the Bannock Burn, a military élite contended for control of a kingdom, and that is not quite the same thing as Scotland fighting against England. The other purpose in listing these biographies is to show that many of these deadly enemies on the day were in fact related, knew each other, and had sometimes even been of help to each other in the past.

KING ROBERT I

The ancestry of Robert Bruce was an unusual hybrid and his Norman and Gaelic upbringing continually sustained him in his long campaign to establish himself as king. Not only was he descended from Henry I of England, related to the de Clare family who held the earldoms of Pembroke and later of Gloucester and Hertford, he was also the son of Marjorie of Carrick, a thoroughly Celtic noblewoman from a thoroughly Celtic part of Scotland. And Bruce's first wife, Isabella, was a scion of the Gaelic-speaking house of Mar in north-eastern Scotland. She was the mother of Princess Marjorie, a woman who would have a vital part to play in the perpetuation of the dynasty, albeit under another name. Isabella died in 1296. From an early age, the future king was almost certainly trilingual in Gaelic, Scots and Norman French. The Bruce surname may derive from Brix, rendered as de Brix, a place in the Cotentin Peninsula to the west of Normandy. Although he held land in County Durham, Essex and Middlesex, the power base of the future Scots king was in the Scottish south-west, in the lordship of Annandale and the earldom of Carrick. He was probably born at the castle at Turnberry. Bruce fathered five legitimate children and acknowledged six illegitimate others. But only David, who succeeded as King of Scotland and reigned until 1371, survived to any great age. He was the son of the king's second marriage, to Elizabeth de Burgh, the daughter of Richard Og de Burgh, Earl of Ulster, a close friend of Edward I of England.

KING EDWARD II

As the fourth son and eleventh child of Edward I and Eleanor of Castile, it was unlikely that Edward would become king. But following the death of his elder brother, who carried the unlikely name of Alphonso, he became the heir apparent. With Isabella of France, he managed to father at least five children. One was to become a future Queen of Scotland. Known as Joan of the

Tower (she was born in the Tower of London), she married David II, the son of King Robert I. Edward appears to have been bisexual, for not only did he fulfil his dynastic duties on four occasions with his queen, he also had an illegimate son, Adam Fitzroy, his surname acknowledging his royal parentage. Adam was therefore not the product of obligation. But it is for his reckless homosexual affairs that Edward is remembered, first with Piers Gaveston and then with Hugh Despenser. Sandwiched between the reigns of two powerful Plantagenet kings in the shape of his father, Edward I, and his son, Edward III, Edward II was always going to suffer by comparison. But historians are united in characterising his rule of England as disastrous.

EDWARD BRUCE

Always ambitious, energetic and sometimes impetuous, Edward led an invasion of Ireland and in 1315, only a year after Bannockburn, had himself proclaimed as High King of Ireland. This was not as unlikely as it may seem. The second or third son of Robert Bruce, Earl of Carrick (Robert being the eldest), Edward was probably sent to be fostered in Antrim, fosterage being an ancient Gaelic tradition. And he had Irish royal blood in his ancestry, the blood of high kings, including the far-famed Brian Boru. But his reign in Ireland was short-lived, ending in 1318 at the Battle of Faughart by defeat and death at the hands of the army led by Sir John de Bermingham, a relative of the Bruces through Queen Elizabeth of Scotland. That meant that of five Bruce brothers, Robert, Edward, Niall, Alexander and Thomas, only one survived into anything like old age.

GILBERT DE CLARE, EARL OF GLOUCESTER

The grandson of Edward I and nephew of Edward II, Gilbert was powerful, the 8th Earl of Gloucester and 7th Earl of Hertford and the husband of Maud de Burgh, who was the sister of Queen Elizabeth of Scotland. That meant he was King Robert's brother-in-law. After his death at Bannockburn, the Scots king kept vigil with a man who was a close relative. Gloucester and Maud de Burgh had no children and the wealthy earldoms were split between her sisters, Eleanor, Margaret and Elizabeth. They were all married to Edward II's favourites, Hugh Despenser, Hugh de Audley and Roger d'Amory. Gloucester was at the centre of a web of connections that pulled loyalties in at least two directions, and one of them was always to family advantage and the acquisition of land.

JAMES DOUGLAS

Standing not quite outside this web but on its periphery was James Douglas, Bruce's greatest commander. The eldest son of Sir William Douglas, his inheritance in Douglasdale had been seized by Sir Robert Clifford and through his alliance with Bruce he hoped to regain his ancestral lands. A brilliant and daring soldier, he seems not to have found time for formal marriage and had two children by unknown mothers. William Douglas died in 1333 at the disastrous battle at Halidon Hill near Berwick upon Tweed and was succeeded by his half-brother, a man to whom history has been unkind. He was known as Hugh the Dull. No doubt by comparison with James he was, but nevertheless he was the progenitor of a powerful dynasty of Douglas earls – who were anything but dull.

HUMPHREY DE BOHUN, EARL OF HEREFORD

His marriage to Elizabeth, daughter of Edward I, made de Bohun Edward II's brother-in-law and his capture and ransom after Bannockburn triggered royal traffic in two directions. Earl Humphrey was wealthy but instead of cash, King Robert traded him for Queen Elizabeth, Princess Marjorie, Bishop Wishart and Bishop Lamberton. As most of the English magnates did, de Bohun eventually opposed Edward II and fought his army at the Battle of Boroughbridge in 1322. He seems to have suffered an appallingly painful death. Fighting on a bridge, he was skewered by a pike thrust up through the planks by a pikeman standing in the river. As the man twisted and pushed the weapon, de Bohun's screams heralded defeat for the rebel army.

THOMAS RANDOLPH, EARL OF MORAY

The precise lines of descent are unclear but Randolph may have been Robert Bruce's nephew. He certainly married Isabel Stewart of Bonkyll whose brother, Sir John, was killed fighting alongside William Wallace at Falkirk 1298. Recent DNA research has shown that Sir John Stewart of Bonkyll was the undoubted progenitor of the Stewart dynasty. Randolph was at Scone to support the coronation of King Robert but after his capture at the Battle of Methven, he changed sides. And then when he was captured by Bruce, it may well have been family connections that saved his neck and saw him come once more into the king's camp. He played a key role at Bannockburn.

SIR HENRY DE BOHUN

The nephew of Earl Humphrey de Bohun, he famously died at the hands of King Robert on the first day at Bannockburn as he 'missit the nobill kyng' in Barbour's phrase. Through Hereford, Sir Henry was related to Edward II and was reputedly close to Elizabeth, Earl Humphrey's royal wife.

WALTER STEWART

Only 18 years old at Bannockburn, he shared command of his brigade with the much more experienced James Douglas. As the sixth hereditary High Steward of Scotland, his role became his surname and with an important marriage, the surname of a dynasty of kings and queens. His stepmother was the daughter of Walter de Burgh, the first Earl of Ulster and the grandfather of Bruce's Queen Elizabeth, and his natural mother was Cecilia of Dunbar, the sister of Earl Patrick who helped Edward II escape after his defeat at Bannockburn.

AYMER DE VALENCE, EARL OF PEMBROKE

He had no children but his name is remembered through his wife's foundation of Pembroke College, Cambridge. A constant supporter of Edward II, despite the insults hurled by Piers Gaveston, de Valence also had strong connections to the French royal family. He held lands in the Calais and Poitou regions of France. Probably the most competent English soldier at Bannockburn and, having fought Bruce twice at Methven and Loudoun Hill, he also had experience, but his advice appears to have been ignored. In 1317 he was captured while on diplomatic business in France and his ransom of £10,000 destroyed the family finances.

SIR ROBERT KEITH

Bearing the title of Marischal of Scotland, which had been bestowed on his ancestors by King Malcolm IV, his official duties were the protection of the king's person at parliament, and the Scottish regalia (although most of this had been removed by Edward I). Keith led the Scottish cavalry at Bannockburn and went on to take an active role in the government of Robert I. He was killed in 1332 at the battle of Dupplin Moor by a force led by Edward Balliol, the son of the deposed King John. They were the Disinherited, lords who had been deprived of their lands after Bannockburn because of their support for the cause of Edward II.

SIR HENRY BEAUMONT

He fought in every major battle in Scotland for the 35 years from Falkirk in 1298 to the Battle of Halidon Hill in 1333. Despite his apparent bone-headed insistence in repeatedly charging Randolph's schiltron at Bannockburn, Beaumont developed the deadly archery tactics which won victories at Dupplin Moor for the Disinherited and at Halidon Hill for Edward III. These involved intensive volleys. Skilled archers standing in formation could shoot so fast that they had several arrows in the air at any one time and these tactics were developed to devastating effect in the Hundred Years War in France. In 1310 Sir Henry became the

Earl of Buchan by marriage and his motivation to fight so doggedly in Scotland was the retrieval of the earldom. But he also had strong French connections and some of these could be exotic: Beaumont was the grandson of John de Brienne, King of the Crusader state of Jerusalem.

QUEEN ELIZABETH OF SCOTLAND

King Robert's second wife was released from a long captivity after Bannockburn and after the coronation of 1306, she reigned until 1327. But despite a long time as Queen of Scotland, she appears to have been written out of history, or at least popular history. When Queen Elizabeth II of Great Britain and Northern Ireland was crowned in 1953 and the Royal Mail postboxes with her name and regnal number were set up in Scotland, there was uproar. Zealots cried that there may have been an Elizabeth I in England but the new queen was not the second of that name to reign in Scotland but the first. They appear to have forgotten King Robert's brave queen.

SIR ROBERT CLIFFORD

This tough and experienced soldier knew Scotland well. He was appointed Lord Warden of the Marches and Governor of Carlisle Castle and had a direct personal interest in quelling the Scots, and in particular their cross-border raiding. Clifford was heir to the vast Westmorland lands of the Anglo-Norman Vieux-pont family (later rendered as Vipont) as well as holdings around Skipton in Yorkshire. He fought in the victory at Falkirk but along with Gilbert de Clare, Earl of Gloucester, was killed at

Bannockburn. Through his marriage to Maud de Clare, he was related not only to Gilbert but also King Robert.

ISABELLA, COUNTESS OF BUCHAN

Surely one of the bravest of all who were closely involved in the campaigns leading up to Bannockburn, Isabella was confined and humiliated in a cage slung over the walls of Berwick Castle in punishment for her key role in crowning Bruce. She was married to John Comyn, Earl of Buchan, who supported the claims of Edward II. But in fact Isabella had close ties with the forces opposed to Bruce in 1314. Through her mother, Johanna de Clare, she was part of the Gloucester network. After four years of suffering in the cage, Isabella was moved to the Carmelite Friary in Berwick but when Bruce's other female relatives were exchanged for the captured Earl of Hereford, there was no mention of the Countess of Buchan. She may have died of the effects of prolonged exposure before then.

SIR THOMAS GREY

Like Sir Robert Clifford, Grey was an English Borderer who knew Scotland well. From Heaton in Northumberland, he fought in Scotland in the campaigns of Edward I and was captured in 1303 at Melrose Abbey by the Scots. On his release a year later, he rescued Sir Henry Beaumont at Stirling and despite their squabble on the first day of the battle at Bannockburn, these men had a history as comrades-in-arms. Grey was appointed Constable of Norham Castle, a formidable fortress on the Tweed and the Scottish border, and in later life he recounted tales of the battle at Bannockburn to his son, also Sir Thomas Grey, which formed part of the *Scalachronica*, a record of the reigns of Edwards I, II and III.

SIR ALEXANDER SETON

Although he attended King Robert's coronation in 1306, Seton was in the English camp at Bannockburn – at least for the first night. In 1320 he signed the Declaration of Arbroath and in 1327 was appointed Keeper of Berwick. When the town was besieged by Edward III's army, Seton negotiated an agreement that the town would surrender unless it was relieved after a certain period, somewhat like the arrangements made at Stirling Castle in 1313/14. As surety, Seton gave his son, Thomas, as a hostage. When William Keith took over Berwick, he refused to surrender and the English hanged Thomas Seton in front of the town wall. His father later witnessed the granting of Berwick to the English crown.

HUGH DESPENSER

Yet another in the wider Gloucester circle, he married Eleanor de Clare as a settlement for a debt of 2,000 marks owed to his father by Edward I. It was to prove a fruitful match when Gilbert de Clare was killed at Bannockburn. The dead man had no children and his vast holdings were divided between his sisters and their husbands. Instead of installing his furniture in the castle of a Scottish lordship, the outcome of the battle made Despenser a tremendously wealthy magnate in the south-west of England and in Glamorgan. He became the lover of Edward II (the chronicler,

Jean Froissart, called him a sodomite) and like Piers Gaveston became the enemy of the great magnates. After capture in 1326, he suffered a horrific death with biblical verses denouncing arrogance and evil carved into his skin, hanging, castration and disembowelling before he was finally beheaded.

AONGHAS OG MACDONALD OF ISLAY

Chief of Clan Donald and Lord of Islay, Aonghas Og, Young Angus, was a steadfast ally of Robert Bruce and in the dark days after the defeat at Methven may have hidden the fugitive king on the island of Rathlin. At the outset of the fourteenth century Clan Donald was the junior line that descended from the great Somerled, the first Lord of the Isles. Clan MacDougall was the senior line but they supported King John Balliol and its chiefs were enemies of Bruce. After Bannockburn, the bulk of their lands were granted to Aonghas Og. He became Lord of Lochaber, Durrour and Glencoe, and controlled the islands of Tiree, Mull, Jura and Coll. This transfer of wealth and power laid the basis of the primacy of Clan Donald and its chiefs prospered until the fall of the Lordship of the Isles at the end of the fifteenth century.

SIR MARMADUKE DE THWENG

Wonderfully named, this English knight may be seen as a polar contrast with Aonghas Og. But in fact Marmaduke is far from being the epitome of upper-class Englishness, for it is a Celtic name. Meaning the Servant of Maedoc, an Irish saint of the sixth century, it has come to have comical connotations, bringing upper-crust dimwits to mind. But in fact Sir Marmaduke de Thweng was a tough and resourceful soldier. When William Wallace's and Andrew Moray's army had trapped about 100 English knights and many footsoldiers on the wrong side of Stirling Bridge in 1297 and began to slaughter them, de Thweng was the only knight to cut his way out of the trap and escape. In the aftermath of Bannockburn, the canny old veteran made sure he surrendered only to King Robert. It was said that the king invited the English knight to dine with him and sent him back to Yorkshire laden with gifts rather than holding him to ransom. And the reason for such magnanimity was of course family and feudal ties. De Thweng was the husband of Lucy de Brus, a distant cousin of the Scots king, as well as being a vassal of his father, the 6th Lord of Annandale, for his Yorkshire lands.

ROBERT WISHART, BISHOP OF GLASGOW

Despite a surname that sounds quintessentially Scots, Wishart had Anglo-Norman origins and he was part of the same ruling elite as Bruce and many of his magnates. Like other prelates, Wishart saw the independence of the Scottish Crown and the Scottish Church as inextricably linked. But his support for King Robert was fierce and uncompromising. With eight years of harsh imprisonment in England and the loss of his sight, Wishart paid the price for his stance but although an old man by that time, perhaps in his mid 60s, he lived long enough to be told of the victory at Bannockburn.

SIR PHILIP MOUBRAY

A Scots nobleman with strong connections in England, Moubray's allegiance to Edward II sprang from family links. His mother was a daughter of John Comyn. But when Bannockburn was decided, Moubray immediately changed sides, apparently without rancour, and he joined Edward Bruce in his quest to become High King of Ireland. But like Bruce, he was killed at the Battle of Faughart in 1318. He married Eve, Lady Redcastle, a Forfarshire noblewoman.

WILLIAM LAMBERTON, BISHOP OF ST ANDREWS

Originally from Lamberton in Berwickshire, close to the English border, the Bishop of St Andrews was a protégé of Robert Wishart and his election at the age of perhaps 27 or 28 was surprising. It may have been forced through by William Wallace, who knew the young priest's position on the independence of the Scottish Crown and Church. In 1304, while both men supported Edward I, Lamberton and Bruce formed a compact of mutual support at Stirling. With Robert Wishart, he was arrested in 1306 but after the accession of Edward II, he swore fealty to the new king. In 1309 he was acting as an envoy in negotiations on behalf of the English king. It is difficult to work out which side he was on but by 1312, Lamberton was certainly supporting Bruce. In 1321 he succeeded in having the sentences of excommunication on him and his king lifted.

RAOUL DE MONTHERMER

Or Ralph de Monthermer. A fascinating, charismatic character, he was an Anglo-French knight in the household of Joan of Acre, a daughter of Edward I. When her husband, Gilbert de Clare, Earl of Gloucester and Hertford, died in 1295, Joan fell in love with Raoul and married him in secret. Incandescent, Edward I threw the young knight in prison but with the help of Anthony Bek, the warrior-bishop of Durham who was also a trusted advisor to the old king, Joan persuaded her father to release him. Raoul must have been charming or impressive or both for Edward I allowed him to take the ducal titles during his wife's lifetime. In 1306 he warned Bruce that the old king was planning to have him arrested for treason and so eight years later, after Bannockburn, the Scots king returned the favour and released the captured Raoul without ransom.

MARJORIE BRUCE

In a short life of only 19 years, King Robert's daughter nevertheless occupied a pivotal role in Scotland's history. When she returned from long imprisonment in England in 1314, Marjorie married Walter Stewart, the sixth High Steward of Scotland. In 1316, while heavily pregnant, the young princess was thrown from her horse near Paisley. After a premature labour, she died but her child survived. The little boy was to succeed his Uncle David in 1371 and become Robert II of Scotland, the first Stewart king and the ancestor of many monarchs.

Appendix 3
The Sources

Bannockburn was an event of such moment and its outcome so unexpected that it was widely reported. Three of the most informative and colourful primary sources are appended here. Both the *Lanercost Chronicle* from the Priory at Lanercost in north Cumberland and the *Scalachronica* of Sir Thomas Grey from north Northumberland are English accounts, but they were compiled from the testimony of eyewitnesses and each was written close to the border. Consequently, their authors were well-informed about Scotland and the doings of King Robert and his captains. John Barbour's great epic, 'The Bruce', was composed 60 years after the battle but it also appears to rely on eyewitness evidence. However, it must be borne in mind that it is a considerable piece of art and there are on occasion flights of artistic licence, especially where numbers are concerned. Nevertheless, it feels reliable, has the smit of authenticity. And it was written with tremendous verve.

The Chronicle of Lanercost, 1272–1346

An Excerpt

In winter, about the feast of S. Martin, to wit, on the feast day of S. Bricius, a first-born son was born and was named Edward, like his father and grandfather.

Now the oft-mentioned Robert, seeing that thus he had the whole March of England under tribute, applied all his thoughts to getting possession of the town of Berwick, which was in the King of England's hands. Coming unexpectedly to the castle on the night of S. Nicholas, he laid ladders against the walls and began to scale them; and had not a dog betrayed the approach of the Scots by loud barking, it is believed that he would quickly have taken the castle and, in consequence, the town.

Now these ladders which they placed against the walls were of wonderful construction, as I myself, who write these lines, beheld with my own eyes. For the Scots had made two strong ropes as long as the height of the wall, making a knot at one end of each cord. They had made a wooden board also, about two feet and a half long and half a foot broad, strong enough to carry a man, and in the two extremities of the board they had made two holes, through which the two ropes could be passed; then the cords, having been passed through as far as the knots, they had made two other knots in the ropes one foot and a half higher, and above these knots they placed another log or board, and so on to the end of the ropes. They had also made an iron hook, measuring at least one foot along one limb, and this was to lie over the wall; but the other limb, being of the same length, hung downwards towards the ground, having at its end a round hole wherein the point of a lance could be inserted, and two rings on the two sides wherein the said ropes could be knotted.

Having fitted them together in this manner, they took a strong spear as long as the height of the wall, placing the point thereof in the iron hole, and two men lifted the ropes and boards with that spear and placed the iron hook (which was not a round one) over the wall. Then they were able to climb up by those wooden steps just as one usually climbs ordinary ladders, and the greater the weight of the climber the more firmly the iron hook clung over the wall. But lest the ropes should lie too close to the wall and hinder the ascent, they had made fenders round every third step which thrust the ropes off the wall. When, therefore, they had placed two ladders upon the wall, the dog betrayed them as I have said, and they left the ladders there, which our people next day hung upon a pillory to put them to shame. And thus a dog saved the town on that occasion, just as of old geese saved Rome by their gaggle, as saith S. Augustine in *de Civitate Dei.*

Robert, having failed in his attempt on Berwick, marched with his army to the town of S. John, which was then still in the King of England's hands; and he laid siege thereto, and on Monday of the octave of Epiphany it was taken by the Scots, who scaled the walls by night on ladders, and entered the town through the negligence of sentries and guards. Next day Robert caused those citizens of the better class who were of the Scottish nation to be killed, but the English were allowed to go away free. But the Scottish Sir William Oliphant, who had long time held that town for the King of England against the Scots, was bound and sent far away to the Isles. The town itself the Scots utterly destroyed.

After the feast of the Nativity of S. John the Baptist, when the English truce on the March had lapsed, Robert de Brus threatened to invade England in his usual manner. The people of Northumberland, Westmorland and Cumberland, and other Borderers, apprehending this, and neither having nor hoping for any defence or help from their king (seeing that he was engaged in distant parts of England, seeming not to give them a thought), offered to the said Robert no small sum of money, indeed a very large one, for a truce to last till the feast of S. Michael in the following year.

All this time the body of Piers de Gaveston remained above ground unburied with the Friars Preachers of Oxford, who daily said for his soul a placebo, a dirige, and a mass with nones, receiving from the king half a mark for their trouble.

In the same year about the feast of the Assumption of the Blessed Virgin, the Emperor was poisoned, as was said, by a certain monk.

After the feast of S. Michael, the king caused the earls and barons to be summoned to parliament in

London, and there an agreement, such as it was, was made between them on Sunday next before the feast of S. Luke, and they made to him such an humbling and obeisance as befitted a king, which afterwards they did not observe.

Now at the beginning of Lent, the Scots cunningly entered the castle of Roxburgh at night by ladders, and captured all the castle except one tower, wherein the warden of the castle, Sir Gillemin de Fiennes, a knight of Gascony, had taken refuge with difficulty, and his people with him; but the Scots got possession of that tower soon afterwards. And they razed to the ground the whole of that beautiful castle, just as they did other castles which they succeeded in taking, lest the English should ever hereafter be able to lord it over the land through holding the castles.

In the same season of Lent they captured Edinburgh Castle in the following manner. In the evening one day the besiegers of that castle delivered an assault in force upon the south gate, because, owing to the position of the castle there was no other quarter where an assault could be made. Those within gathered together at the gate and offered a stout resistance; but meanwhile the other Scots climbed the rocks on the north side, which was very high and fell away steeply from the foot of the wall. There they laid ladders to the wall and climbed up in such numbers that those within could not withstand them; and thus they threw open the gates, admitted their comrades, got possession of the whole castle and killed the English. They razed the said castle to the ground, just as they had done to Roxburgh Castle.

Having accomplished this success, they marched to Stirling and besieged that castle with their army. In the

† same year died Sir Thomas de Multan, Lord of Gillesland, on the sixth of the kalends of December, leaving an only daughter as his heir, named Margaret, whom Robert de Clifford, son of Robert of the same name, married at HofFe [House of Fe] in the seventh year of her age, he himself lying on his bed. And in the life of the said Robert, Ralph de Dacre, son of Sir William de Dacre, married the same Margaret, having a right to her through a contract concluded between Thomas de Multan, father of the said Margaret, and William de Dacre, before her former marriage.

On Tuesday after the octave of Easter, Edward de Brus, Robert's brother, invaded England by way of Carlisle with an army, contrary to agreement, and remained there three days at the bishop's manor house, to wit, at Rose, and sent a strong detachment of his army to burn the southern and western districts during those three days. They burnt many towns and two churches, taking men and women prisoners, and collected a great number of cattle in Inglewood Forest and elsewhere, driving them off with them on the Friday; they killed few men except those who made determined resistance; but they made attack upon the city of Carlisle because of the knights and country people who were assembled there. Now the Scots did all these wrongs at that time because the men of that March had not paid them the tribute which they had pledged themselves to pay on certain days. Although the Scots had hostages from the sons and heirs of the knights of that country in full security for covenanted sums, yet they did not on that account refrain from committing the aforesaid wrongs.

† Now about the feast of Pentecost, the King of England approached the March of Scotland; also the Earl of Gloucester, the Earl of Hereford, the Earl of Pembroke, and the Earl of Angus, Sir Robert de Clifford, Sir John Comyn (son of the murdered John), Sir Henry de Beaumont, Sir John de Segrave, Sir Pagan de Typtoft, Sir Edmund de Mauley, Sir Ingelram de Umfraville, with other barons, knights, and a splendid and numerous army, if only they had had the Lord as ally. But the Earl of Lancaster and the other English earls who were of his party remained at home with their men (except those with whom they were bound in strict obligation to furnish the king in war), because the king as yet had refused to agree with them or to perform what he had promised before. And whereas when his noble father Edward went on a campaign in Scotland, he used to visit on his march [the shrines of] the English saints, Thomas of Canterbury, Edmund, Hugh, William, and Cuthbert, offering fair oblations, commending himself to their prayers, and also bestowing liberal gifts to monasteries and the poor, this [king] did none of these things; but marching with great pomp and elaborate state, he took goods from the monasteries on his journey, and, as was reported, did and said things to the prejudice and injury of the saints. In consequence of this and other things it is not surprising that confusion and everlasting shame overtook him and his army, which was foretold at the time by certain religious men of England.

Thus before the feast of the Nativity of S. John the Baptist, the king, having massed his army, advanced with the aforesaid pomp towards Stirling Castle, to relieve it

from siege and to engage the Scots, who were assembled there in all their strength. On the vigil of the aforesaid Nativity, the king's army arrived after dinner near Torwood; and, upon information that there were Scots in the wood, the king's advanced guard, commanded by Lord de Clifford, began to make a circuit of the wood to prevent the Scots escaping by flight. The Scots did not interfere until they [the English] were far ahead of the main body, when they showed themselves, and, cutting off the king's advanced guard from the middle and rear columns, they charged and killed some of them and put the rest to flight. From that moment began a panic among the English and the Scots grew bolder.

On the morrow – an evil, miserable and calamitous day for the English – when both sides had made themselves ready for battle, the English archers were thrown forward before the line, and the Scottish archers engaged them, a few being killed and wounded on either side; but the King of England's archers quickly put the others to flight. Now when the two armies had approached very near each other, all the Scots fell on their knees to repeat Pater noster, commending themselves to God and seeking help from heaven; after which they advanced boldly against the English. They had so arranged their army that two columns went abreast in advance of the third, so that neither should be in advance of the other; and the third followed, in which was Robert. Of a truth, when both armies engaged each other, and the great horses of the English charged the pikes of the Scots, as it were into a dense forest, there arose a great and terrible crash of spears broken and of destriers wounded to the death; and so they remained without movement for a while. Now the English in the rear could not reach the Scots because the leading division was in the way, nor could they do anything to help themselves, wherefore there was nothing for it but to take to flight. This account I heard from a trustworthy person who was present as eye-witness.

In the leading division were killed the Earl of Gloucester, Sir John Comyn, Sir Pagan de Typtoft, Sir Edmund de Mauley and many other nobles, besides foot soldiers who fell in great numbers. Another calamity which befell the English was that, whereas they had shortly before crossed a great ditch called Bannockburn, into which the tide flows, and now wanted to recross it in confusion, many nobles and others fell into it with their horses in the crush, while others escaped with much difficulty, and many were never able to extricate themselves from the ditch; thus Bannockburn was spoken about for many years in English throats.

The king and Sir Hugh le Despenser (who, after Piers de Gaveston, was as his right eye) and Sir Henry de Beaumont (whom he had promoted to an earldom in Scotland), with many others mounted and on foot, to their perpetual shame fled like miserable wretches to Dunbar Castle, guided by a certain knight of Scotland who knew through what districts they could escape. Some who were not so speedy in flight were killed by the Scots, who pursued them hotly; but these, holding bravely together, came safe and sound through the ambushes into England. At Dunbar the king embarked with some of his chosen

followers in an open boat for Berwick, leaving all the others to their fate.

In like manner as the king and his following fled in one direction to Berwick, so the Earl of Hereford, the Earl of Angus, Sir John de Segrave, Sir Antony de Lucy and Sir Ingelram de Umfraville, with a great crowd of knights, six hundred other mounted men and one thousand foot, fled in another direction towards Carlisle. The Earl of Pembroke left the army on foot and saved himself with the fugitive Welsh; but the aforesaid earls and others, who had fled towards Carlisle were captured on the way at Bothwell Castle, for the sheriff, the warden of the castle, who had held the castle down to that time for the King of England, perceiving that his countrymen had won the battle, allowed the chief men who came thither to enter the castle in the belief that they would find a safe refuge, and when they had entered he took them prisoners, thereby treacherously deceiving them. Many, also, were taken wandering round the castle and hither and thither in the country, and many were killed; it was said, also, that certain knights were captured by women, nor did any of them get back to England save in abject confusion. The Earl of Hereford, the Earl of Angus, Sir [John] de Segrave, Sir Antony de Lucy, Sir Ingelram de Umfraville and the other nobles who were in the castle were brought before Robert de Brus and sent into captivity, and after a lengthy imprisonment were ransomed for much money. After the aforesaid victory Robert de Brus was commonly called King of Scotland by all men, because he had acquired Scotland by force of arms.

The Scalachronica

The Reigns of Edward I, Edward II and Edward III as Recorded by Sir Thomas Grey

The said King Edward planned an expedition to these parts, where, in [attempting] the relief of the castle of Stirling, he was defeated, and a great number of his people were slain, [including] the Earl of Gloucester and other right noble persons; and the Earl of Hereford was taken at Bothwell, whither he had beaten retreat, where he was betrayed by the governor. He was released [in exchange] for the wife of Robert de Brus and the Bishop of St. Andrews.

As to the manner in which this discomfiture befell, the chronicles explain that after the Earl of Atholl had captured the town of St John [Perth] for the use of Robert de Brus from William Oliphant, captain [thereof] for the King of England, being at that time an adherent of his [Edward's], although shortly after he deserted him, the said Robert marched in force before the castle of Stirling, where Philip de Moubray, knight, having command of the said castle for the King of England, made terms with the said Robert de Brus to surrender the said castle, which he had besieged, unless he [de Moubray] should be relieved: that is, unless the English army came within three leagues of the said castle within eight days of Saint John's day in the summer next to come, he would surrender the said castle. The said King of England came thither for that reason, where the said constable Philip met him at three leagues from the castle, on Sunday the vigil of Saint John, and told him that there was no occasion for him to approach any nearer, for he considered himself as relieved. Then he told him how the enemy had blocked the narrow roads in the forest.

[But] the young troops would by no means stop, but held their way. The advanced guard, whereof the Earl of Gloucester had command, entered the road within the Park, where they were immediately received roughly by the Scots who had occupied the passage. Here Peris de Mountforth, knight, was slain with an axe by the hand of Robert de Brus, as was reported.

While the said advanced guard were following this road, Robert Lord de Clifford and Henry de Beaumont, with three hundred men-at-arms, made a circuit upon the other side of the wood towards the castle, keeping the open ground. Thomas Randolph, Earl of Moray, Robert de Brus's nephew, who was leader of the Scottish advanced guard, hearing that his uncle had repulsed the advanced guard of the English on the other side of the wood, thought that he must have his share, and issuing from the wood with his division marched across the open ground towards the two aforenamed lords.

Sir Henry de Beaumont called to his men: 'Let us wait a little; let them come on; give them room!'

'Sir,' said Sir Thomas Gray, 'I doubt that whatever you give them now, they will have all too soon.'

'Very well!' exclaimed the said Henry, 'if you are afraid, be off!'

'Sir,' answered the said Thomas, 'it is not from fear that I shall fly this day.' So saying he spurred in between him [Beaumont] and Sir William Deyncourt, and charged into the thick of the enemy. William was killed, Thomas was taken prisoner, his horse being killed on the pikes, and he himself carried off with them [the Scots] on foot when they marched off, having utterly routed the squadron of the said two lords. Some of whom [the English] fled to the castle, others to the king's army, which having already left the road through the wood had debouched upon a plain near the water of Forth beyond Bannockburn, an evil, deep, wet marsh, where the said English army unharnessed and remained all night, having sadly lost confidence and being too much disaffected by the events of the day.

The Scots in the wood thought they had done well enough for the day, and were on the point of decamping in order to march during the night into the Lennox, a stronger country, when Sir Alexander de Seton, who was in the service of England and had come thither with the King, secretly left the English army, went to Robert de Brus in the wood, and said to him: 'Sir, this is the time if ever you intend to undertake to reconquer Scotland. The English have lost heart and are discouraged, and expect nothing but a sudden, open attack.'

Then he described their condition, and pledged his head, on pain of being hanged and drawn, that if he [Bruce] would attack them on the morrow he would defeat them easily without [much] loss. At whose [Seton's] instigation they [the Scots] resolved to fight, and at sunrise on the morrow marched out of the wood in three divisions of infantry. They directed their course boldly upon the English army, which had been under arms all night, with their horses bitted. They [the English] mounted in great alarm, for they were not accustomed to dismount to fight on foot; whereas the Scots had taken a lesson from the Flemings, who before that had at Courtrai defeated on foot the power of France. The aforesaid Scots came in line of schiltroms, and attacked the English columns, which were jammed together and could not operate against them [the Scots], so direfully were their horses impaled on the pikes. The troops in the English rear fell back upon the ditch of Bannockburn, tumbling one over the other.

The English squadrons being thrown into confusion by the thrust of pikes upon the horses, began to fly. Those who were appointed to [attend upon] the King's rein, perceiving the disaster, led the King by the rein off the field towards the castle, and off he went, though much against the grain. As the Scottish knights, who were on foot, laid hold of the housing of the King's charger in order to stop him, he struck out so vigorously behind him with a mace that there was none whom he touched that he did not fell to the ground.

As those who had the King's rein were thus drawing him always forward, one of them, Giles de Argentin, a famous knight who had lately come over sea from the wars of the Emperor Henry of Luxemburg, said to the king: 'Sire, your rein was committed to me; you are now in safety; there is your castle where your person may be safe. I am not accustomed to fly, nor am I going to begin now. I commend you to God!' Then, setting spurs to his horse, he returned into the mellay, where he was slain.

The King's charger, having been piked, could go no further; so he mounted afresh on a courser and was taken round the Torwood, and [so] through the plains of Lothian. Those who went with him were saved; all the rest came to grief. The King escaped with great difficulty, travelling thence to Dunbar, where Patrick, Earl of March, received him honourably, and put his castle at his disposal, and even evacuated the place, removing all his people, so that there might be neither doubt nor suspicion that he would do nothing short of his devoir to his lord, for at that time he [Dunbar] was his liegeman. Thence the King went by sea to Berwick and afterwards to the south.

The Bruce

by John Barbour, with a translation by A.A.M. Duncan

Book 12

497 Thus war thai boune on ather sid,
And Inglismen with mekill prid
That war intill thar avaward
500 To the bataill that Schyr Edward
Governyt and led held straucht thar way
The hors with spuris hardnyt thai
And prikyt apon thaim sturdely,
And thai met thaim rycht hardely
505 Sua that at thar assemble thar
Sic a fruschyng of speris war
That fer away men mycht it her.
At that meting foroutyn wer
War stedis stekyt mony ane
510 And mony gude man borne doune and slayne,
And mony ane hardyment douchtely
Was thar eschevyt, for hardely
Thai dang on other with wapnys ser.
Sum of the hors that stekyt wer
515 Ruschyt and relyt rycht rudlye,
Bot the remanand nocht-forthi

That mycht cum to the assembling
For that led maid na stinting
Bot assemblyt full hardely,
520 And thai met thaim full sturdely
With speris that wer scharp to scher
And axys that weile groundyn wer
Quhar-with was roucht mony a rout.
The fechting wes thar sa fell and stout
525 That mony a worthi man and wicht
Throu fors wes fellyt in that fycht
That had na mycht to rys agane.
The Scottismen fast gan thaim payn
Thar fayis mekill mycht to rus,
530 I trow thai sall na payn refuse
Na perell quhill thar fayis be
Set in weill hard perplexité.

[Moray's men attack the main English host]

And quhen the erle of Murref swa
Thar vaward saw sa stoutly ga
535 The way to Schyr Edward all straucht
That met thaim with full mekill maucht,
He held hys way with his baner
To the gret rout quhar samyn wer
The nyne bataillis that war sa braid,
540 That sa fele baneris with thaim haid
And of men sa gret quantité
That it war wonder for to se.
The gud erle thidder tuk the way

With his battaill in gud aray
545 And assemblit sa hardily
That men mycht her that had bene by
A gret frusch of the speris that brast,
For thar fayis assemblyt fast
That on stedis with mekill prid
550 Come prikand as thai wald our-rid
The erle and all his cumpany,
Bot thai met thaim sa sturdely
That mony of thaim till erd thai bar,
For mony a sted was stekyt thar
555 And mony gud man fellyt under fet
That had na hap to rys up yete.
Thar mycht men se a hard bataill
And sum defend and sum assaile
And mony a reale romble rid
560 Be roucht thar apon ather sid
Quhill throu the byrnys bryst the blud
That till erd doune stremand yhude.
The erle of Murreff and his men
Sa stoutly thaim contenyt then
565 That thai wan place ay mar and mar
On thar fayis the-quhether thai war
Ay ten far ane or may perfay,
Sua that it semyt weill that thai
War tynt amang sa gret menye
570 As thai war plungyt in the se.
And quhen the Inglismen has sene
The erle and all his men bedene
Faucht sa stoutly but effraying

Rycht as thai had nane abasing
575 Thaim pressyt thai with all thar mycht
And thai with speris and swerdis brycht
And axis that rycht scharply schar
Ymyddis the vesag met thaim thar.
Thar mycht men se a stalwart stour
580 And mony men of gret valour
With speris mas and knyffis
And other wapynnys wyssyll thar lyvis
Sua that mony fell doune all dede,
The greys woux with the blud all reid
585 The erle that wycht wes and worthi
And his men faucht sa manlyly
That quha-sa had sene thaim that day
I trow forsuth that thai suld say
That thai suld do thar devor wele
590 Swa that thar fayis suld it fele.

Book 13
[Douglas's division attacks]

Quhen thir twa fyrst bataillis wer
Assemblyt as I said you er,
The Stewart Walter that than was
And the gud lord als of Douglas
5 In a bataill, quhen that thai saw
The erle foroutyn dred or aw
Assembill with his cumpany
On all that folk sa sturdely

For till help him thai held thar way
10 And thar bataill in gud aray,
And assemblyt sa hardely
Besid the erle a litill by
That thar fayis feld thar cummyn wele,
For with wapynnys stalwart of stele
15 Thai dang apon with all thar mycht.
Thar fayis resavyt weile Ik hycht
With swerdis speris and with mase,
The bataill thar sa feloune was
And sua rycht gret spilling of blud
20 That on the erd the flousis stud.
The Scottismen sa weill thaim bar
And sua gret slauchter maid thai thar
And fra sa fele the lyvis revyt
That all the feld bludy wes levyt.
25 That tyme thar thre bataillis wer
All syd be sid fechtand weill ner,
Thar mycht men her mony dynt
And wapynnys apon armuris stynt,
And se tumble knychtis and stedis
30 And mony rich and reale wedis
Defoullyt foully under fete,
Sum held on loft sum tynt the suet.
A lang quhill thus fechtand thai war
That men na noyis mycht her thar,
35 Men hard nocht bot granys and dintis
That slew fyr as men slayis on flyntis,
Thai faucht ilk ane sa egerly
That thai maid nother noyis na cry

Bot dang on other at thar mycht
40 With wapnys that war burnyst brycht.
The arowys als sua thyk thar flaw
That thai mycht say wele that thaim saw
That thai a hidwys schour gan ma,
For quhar thai fell Ik undreta
45 Thai left efter thaim taknyng
That sall ned as I trow leching.

[Sir Robert Keith's cavalry disperses
the English archers]

The Inglis archeris schot sa fast
That mycht thar schot haff ony last
It had bene hard to Scottismen
50 Bot King Robert that wele gan ken
That thar archeris war peralous
And thar schot rycht hard and grevous
Ordanyt forouth the assemblé
Hys marschell with a gret menye,
55 Fyve hunder armyt into stele
That on lycht hors war horsyt welle,
For to pryk amang the archeris
And sua assaile thaim with thar speris
That thai na layser haiff to schut.
60 This marschell that Ik off mute
That Schyr Robert of Keyth was cauld
As Ik befor her has you tauld
Quhen he saw the bataillis sua
Assembill and togidder ga

65 And saw the archeris schoyt stoutly,
With all thaim off his cumpany
In hy apon thaim gan he rid
And ourtuk thaim at a sid,
And ruschyt amang thaim sa rudly
70 Stekand thaim sa dispitously
And in sic fusoun berand doun
And slayand thaim foroutyn ransoun
That thai thaim scalyt everilkane,
And fra that tyme furth thar wes nane
75 That assemblyt schot to ma.
Quhen Scottis archeris saw that thai sua
War rebutyt thai woux hardy
And with all thar mycht schot egrely
Amang the horsmen that thar raid
80 And woundis wid to thaim thai maid
And slew of thaim a full gret dele.
Thai bar thaim hardely and wele
For, fra thar fayis archeris war
Scalyt as I said till you ar
85 That ma na thai war be gret thing
Sua that thai dred nocht thar schoting
Thai woux sa hardy that thaim thocht
Thai suld set all thar fayis at nocht.

[The king addresses his division and commits it to the battle]

The merschell and his cumpany
90 Wes yeit, as till you er said I,

Amang the archeris quhar thai maid
With speris roume quhar that thai raid
And slew all that thai mycht ourta,
And thai wele lychtly mycht do sua
95 For thai had nocht a strak to stynt
Na for to hald agayne a dynt,
And agayne armyt men to fycht
May nakyt men have litill mycht.
Thai scalyt thaim on sic maner
100 That sum to thar gret bataill wer
Withdrawyn thaim in full gret hy
And sum war fled all utrely,
Bot the folk that behind thaim was,
That for thar awne folk had na space
105 Yheyt to cum to the assembling
In agayn smertly gan thai ding
The archeris that thai met fleand
That then war maid sa recreand
That thar hartis war tynt clenly,
110 I trow thai sall nocht scaith gretly
The Scottismen with schot that day.
And the gud King Robert that ay
Wes fillyt off full gret bounte
Saw how that his bataillis thre
115 Sa hardely assemblyt thar
And sa weill in the fycht thaim bar
And sua fast on thair fayis gan ding
That him thocht nane had abaysing
And how the archeris war scalyt then,
120 He was all blyth and till his men

He said, 'Lordingis, now luk that ye
Worthy and off gud covyn be
At thys assemble and hardy,
And assembill sa sturdely
125 That na thing may befor you stand.
Our men ar sa freschly fechtand
That thai thar fayis has contrayit sua
That be thai pressyt, Ik underta,
A litill fastyr, ye sall se
130 That thai discumfyt sone sall be.'
Quhen this wes said thai held thar way
And on ane feld assemblyt thai
Sa stoutly that at thar cummyng
Thar fayis war ruschyt a gret thing.

[A further description of the fighting]

135 Thar mycht men se men felly fycht
And men that worthi war and wycht
Do mony worthi vasselage,
Thai faucht as thai war in a rage,
For quhen the Scottis ynkirly
140 Saw thar fayis sa sturdely
Stand into bataill thaim agayn
With all thar mycht and all thar mayn
Thai layid on as men out of wit
And quhar thai with full strak mycht hyt
145 Thar mycht na armur stynt thar strak.
Thai to-fruschyt that thai mycht ourtak
And with axis sic duschys gave

That thai helmys and hedis clave,
And thar fayis rycht hardely
150 Met thaim and dang on thaim douchtely
With wapnys that war styth of stele.
Thar wes the bataill strikyn wele.
Sa gret dyn thar wes of dyntis
As wapnys apon armur styntis,
155 And off speris sa gret bresting
And sic thrang and sic thrysting,
Sic gyrnyng granyng and sa gret
A noyis as thai gan other beit
And ensenyeys on ilka sid
160 Gevand and takand woundis wid,
That it wes hydwys for to her.
All four thar bataillis with that wer
Fechtand in a frount halyly.
A! mychty God! how douchtely
165 Schyr Edward the Bruce and his men
Amang thar fayis contenyt thaim then
Fechtand in sa gud covyn
Sa hardy worthy and sa fyne
That thar vaward ruschyt was
170 And maugré tharis left the place,
And till thar gret rout to warand
Thai went that tane had apon hand
Sa gret anoy that thai war effrayit
For Scottis that thaim hard assayit
175 That than war in a schiltrum all.
Quha hapnyt into that fycht to fall
I trow agane he suld nocht rys.

Thar mycht men se on mony wys
Hardimentis eschevyt douchtely,
180 And mony that wycht war and hardy
Sone liand undre fete all dede
Quhar all the feld off blud wes red,
Armys and quyntys that thai bar
With blud war sa defoulyt thar
185 That thai mycht nocht descroyit be.
A! mychty God! quha than mycht se
That Stewart Walter and his rout
And the gud Douglas that wes sa stout
Fechtand into that stalwart stour,
190 He suld say that till all honour
Thai war worthi that in that fycht
Sa fast pressyt thar fayis mycht
That thaim ruschyt quhar thai yeid.
Thar men mycht se mony a steid
195 Fleand on stray that lord had nane.
A! Lord! quha then gud tent had tane
Till the gud erle of Murreff
And his that sua gret routis geff
And faucht sa fast in that battaill
200 Tholand sic paynys and travaill
That thai and tharis maid sic debat
That quhar thai come thai maid thaim gat.
Than mycht men her ensenyeis cry
And Scottismen cry hardely,
205 'On thaim, on thaim, on thaim, thai faile.'
With that sa hard thai gan assaile
And slew all that thai mycht ourta,

And the Scottis archeris alsua
Schot amang thaim sa deliverly
210 Engrevand thaim sa gretumly
That quhat for thaim that with thaim faucht
That sua gret routis to thaim raucht
And pressyt thaim full egrely
And quhat for arowis that felly
215 Mony gret woundis gan thaim ma
And slew fast off thar hors alsua,
That thai wandyst a litill wei.
Thai dred sa gretly then to dey
That thar covyn wes wer and wer,
220 For thaim that fechtand with thaim wer
Set hardyment and strenth and will
And hart and corage als thar-till
And all thar mayne and all thar mycht
To put thaim fully to flycht.

[The men guarding supplies in the Park choose a leader and move towards the battle, dismaying the English]

225 In this tyme that I tell off her
At that bataill on this maner
Wes strykyn quhar on ather party
Thai war fechtand enforcely,
Yomen and swanys and pitaill
230 That in the Park to yeme vittaill
War left, quhen thai wist but lesing
That thar lordis with fell fechting

On thar fayis assemblyt wer,
Ane off thaimselvyn that war thar
235 Capitane off thaim all thai maid,
And schetis that war sumdele brad
Thai festnyt in steid of baneris
Apon lang treys and speris,
And said that thai wald se the fycht
240 And help thar lordis at thar mycht.
Quhen her-till all assentyt wer
In a rout thai assemblit er
Fyften thousand thai war or ma,
And than in gret hy gan thai ga
245 With thar baneris all in a rout
As thai had men bene styth and stout.
Thai come with all that assemblé
Rycht quhill thai mycht the bataill se,
Than all at anys thai gave a cry,
250 'Sla! sla! apon thaim hastily!'
And thar-withall cumand war thai,
Bot thai war wele fer yete away.
And Inglismen that ruschyt war
Throuch fors of fycht as I said ar
255 Quhen thai saw cummand with sic a cry
Towart thaim sic a cumpany
That thaim thocht wele als mony war
As that wes fechtand with thaim thar
And thai befor had nocht thaim sene,
260 Than wit ye weill withoutyn wene
Thai war abaysit sa gretumly
That the best and the mast hardy

That war intill thar ost that day
Wald with thar mensk haf bene away.

[The king presses the enemy harder and some flee]

265 The King Robert be thar relyng
Saw thai war ner at discomfiting
And his ensenye gan hely cry,
Than with thaim off his cumpany
His fayis he pressyt sa fast that thai
270 War intill sa gret effray
That thai left place ay mar and mar,
For the Scottismen that thar war
Quhen thai saw thaim eschew the fycht
Dang on thaim with all thar mycht
275 That thai scalyt thaim in troplys ser
And till discomfitur war ner
And sum off thaim fled all planly,
Bot thai that wycht war and hardy
That schame lettyt to ta the flycht
280 At gret myscheiff mantemyt the fycht
And stythly in the stour gan stand,
And quhen the king of Ingland
Saw his men fley in syndry place,
And saw his fayis rout that was
285 Worthyn sa wycht and sa hardy
That all his folk war halyly
Sa stonayit that thai had na mycht
To stynt thar fayis in the fycht,
He was abaysyt sa gretumly

290 That he and his cumpany
Fyve hunder armyt all at rycht
Intill a frusch all tok the flycht
And to the castell held thar way,
And yeit haiff Ik hard som men say
295 That off Valence Schir Aymer
Quhen he the feld saw vencusyt ner
Be the reyngye led away the king
Agayne his will fra the fechting.
And quhen Schyr Gylis the Argenté
300 Saw the king thus and his menye
Schap thaim to fley sa spedyly,
He come rycht to the king in hy
And said, 'Schyr, sen it is sua
That ye thusgat your gat will ga
305 Havys gud day for agayne will I,
Yeit fled I never sekyrly
And I cheys her to bid and dey
Than for to lyve schamly and fley.'
His bridill but mar abad
310 He turnyt and agayne he rade
And on Edward the Bruys rout
That wes sa sturdy and sa stout
As drede off nakyn thing had he
He prikyt, cryand, 'the Argenté,'
315 And thai with speris sua him met
And sua fele speris on him set
That he and hors war chargyt sua
That bathe till the erd gan ga
And in that place thar slane wes he.

320 Off hys deid wes rycht gret pité,
He wes the thrid best knycht perfay
That men wyst lyvand in his day,
He did mony a fayr journé.
On Saryzynys thre derenyeys faucht he
325 And intill ilk derenye off tha
He vencussyt Saryzynnys twa.
His gret worschip tuk thar ending.

[The English army scatters; many are drowned in Bannockburn or are killed by Scots]

And fra Schyr Aymer with the king
Was fled wes nane that durst abid
330 Bot fled scalyt on ilka sid,
And thar fayis thaim pressyt fast.
Thai war to say suth sua agast
And fled sa fast rycht effrayitly
That off thaim a full gret party
335 Fled to the water of Forth and thar
The mast part off thaim drownyt war,
And Bannokburne betwix the brays
Off men and hors sua stekyt wais
That apon drownyt hors and men
Men mycht pas dry out – our it then.

(497) Thus they were ready on either side. And Englishmen of great pride who were in their vanguard held their way straight to the division that Sir Edward commanded and led. (500) They spurred their horses and galloped at them boldly, and [the Scots]

met them hardily so that at their meeting there was such a smashing of spears that men could hear it far away. (508) At their encounter, not a doubt, many a steed was impaled, and many a good man borne down and killed; and many a valiant deed was done there bravely, for they assaulted each other stoutly with many [kinds of] weapons. (514) Some of the horses that were stabbed reared and fell right roughly. But the rest, nonetheless, who could get to the encounter, did not hold back because of that hindrance, but attacked very strongly. (520) And [the Scots] met them sturdily, with spears that were cutting-sharp, and axes that were well ground, with which many a blow was struck. The fight there was so hard and fierce that many a worthy and brave man was felled in that struggle, and had no strength to rise again. (528) The Scotsmen battled hard to overthrow their enemy's great power. I'm sure they will refuse no effort or danger until their enemies are placed in really great trouble.

(533) And when the earl of Moray saw their vanguard so stoutly take the way straight to Sir Edward, who met them with very great force, he held his way with his banner to the great army, where there were together the nine divisions of such breadth, which had so many banners with them, and with such a quantity of men, that it was remarkable to see. (543) The good earl took the way there with his division in good order, and attacked so strongly that if you had come by you would have heard a great crash of the spears that broke, for their enemies attacked fast, galloping on steeds with great arrogance, as if to ride down the earl and all his company. (552) But [the latter] met them so firmly that they bore many of them down to the earth, for many a horse was impaled there, and many good men felled under their feet had no chance of getting up again. (557) There you could see a

remorseless battle, some defending, some attacking, and many a splendid mighty blow dealt there on both sides, until blood burst through the mail-coat and went streaming down to the earth. (563) The earl of Moray and his men carried themselves so valiantly then that they won more and more ground from their enemies, although [the enemy] was ten or more to [their] one, I'm sure, so that it even seemed that they were lost among so huge a host, like [men] plunged into the sea. (571) And when the Englishmen saw the earl and all his men together fight so stoutly and fearlessly, as if they were not discouraged, they pressed the [Scots] with all their might. And, with bright spears and swords and axes that cut pretty sharply, the [latter] met them there, face to face. (579) There you could see a fierce engagement, and many men of great valour with spears, maces, knives and other weapons, give up their lives, so that many fell down dead; the grass grew red with the blood. (585) The earl, who was valiant and bold, and his men, fought so manfully that anyone who saw them on that day would, I am sure, have said that they did their duty well, so that their foes would feel it.

When these first two divisions had engaged, as I said to you before, the Steward, Walter that is, and also the good lord of Douglas, in one division, when they saw the earl, without fear or dread, with his company, encounter all the [English] folk so sturdily, they held their way to help him with their division, in good array, (11) and clashed so strongly a little way beside the earl, that the enemy certainly felt their arrival, for with strong steel weapons they launched [themselves] on [the English] with all their might. Their foes received [their attack] well, I'm sure, with swords, spears and maces. (18) The battle was so fierce there, [with] such a huge spilling of blood, that pools [of it] formed on the earth. The Scotsmen bore themselves so well, made such great slaughter there and deprived so many of their lives, that the whole field was left bloody. (25) At that time the three divisions were fighting there pretty closely side by side. You could hear many a blow there, and weapons falling on armour, and see knights and horses fall, with lots of rich and flamboyant clothes trampled basely underfoot; some kept on [saddle], some [fell and] lost their lives. (33) They fought like that for a long while, [so] that you could hear no noise there; men heard nothing but grunts and blows, that struck fire as you do striking a flint. (37) They fought each other so intently that they made neither shout nor yell, but struck each other with all their might, with weapons that were burnished bright. The arrows, too, flew so thickly there, that those who saw them could well have said that they made a horrible shower, for wherever they fell, I promise you, they left tokens behind them that needed a leeches treatment.

(47) The English archers fired so fast that if their shooting had persisted, it would have gone hard for the Scotsmen. But King Robert, who knew well what a danger their archers were, [with] their hard and right hurtful shooting, ordered out of the fray his marischal, with a great company, (55) five hundred armed in steel, who were well horsed on light steeds, to gallop among the archers and so attack them with spears, that they would have no opportunity to fire. This marischal that I tell of, who was called Sir Robert Keith, as I've told you before, when he saw the divisions encounter and clash together thus, and saw the archers firing boldly, with [the men] of all his company rode quickly against them, and came upon them at a flank; (69) [he] rode among them so forcefully, spearing them so relentlessly, knocking [them] down and slaying them in such numbers without mercy, that one and all they scattered; from that time on none gathered to try such firing.

(76) When the Scottish archers saw that they had been driven back like that, they grew bold, shot eagerly with all their might among the horsemen who rode there, and made terrible wounds among them, slaying a very great many of them. (82) They behaved boldly and well, for, after the enemy's archers were scattered, as I said to you before, who were more numerous than they were by a large number, so that they did not fear their firing, they grew so bold that they thought they would completely defeat their enemies.

(89) The marischal and his company were still, as I said before, among the archers where they made space with spears where they rode, and slew all that they could overtake. They could do this quite easily because they had no blows to stop nor [had they] to withstand a knock. And unarmed men have little power to fight against those with armour. [The English archers] scattered in such a way that some pulled back in great haste to their great division, and some fled altogether. (103) But the folk who were behind them and who had no space for their own men still to reach the [place of] conflict, soon drove forcibly up against the archers whom they met fleeing, and who were then made so frightened that they clean lost heart; I'm sure that they will not harm the Scots much that day with shooting. (112) And good King Robert, who was always filled with a generous spirit, saw how his three divisions were engaged so strongly there, bore themselves so well in the fighting, and pressed so hard on their foes that he thought none was losing heart, and [saw] how the archers had scattered then, he was very cheerful, and said to his men, (121) 'Lords, now be careful that you are worthy, bold, and of good skills at this fight; and struggle so hard that nothing will withstand you. (126) Our men are fighting so freshly that they have thrown the enemy into such disor-

der that if the [enemy] are pressed a little harder, you'll see that they'll soon be defeated.' When this was said, they held their way and fought on one field so stoutly that when they came upon their foes, [these] were drastically pushed back.

(135) There you could see men fighting for dear life, and men who were worthy and brave do many a courageous act, fighting as though they were in a rage, for when the Scots especially saw their foes standing against them in battle so sturdily, with all their might and main they laid into [them] like men out of their wits. (144) Where they could strike with a full stroke, there no armour could withstand their blow. They cut down those they could overtake, and gave such blows with axes that they split heads and helmets. Their foes met them right boldly and laid into them doughtily with weapons that were of strong steel. (152) The battle was well-fought there. There was such a din of blows, [such] as weapons landing on armour, such a great breaking of spears, such pressure and such pushing, such snarling and groaning, so much noise as they struck the others, and shouted rallying cries on each side, giving and receiving great wounds, that it was horrible to hear. (162) At that all four divisions were fighting altogether on one front. Ah! Mighty God! how bravely Sir Edward Bruce and his men bore themselves among their foes then, (167) fighting in such good spirit, so hardy, worthy and distinguished, that [the English] vanguard was defeated and, in spite of their [men], left the ground going for safety to the great host, which had got into so much trouble that they were dismayed, for the Scots relentlessly attacked them, who were then all in one schiltrum. (176) Whoever chanced to fall in that fighting, I don't think he would get up again! There you could see valiant deeds of many kinds accomplished boldly, and many brave and strong [men] soon

lying dead underfoot, where all the field was red with blood; the arms and coats of arms that they wore were so besmirched with blood there, that they could not be made out. (186) Ah! Mighty God! Anyone who could see Walter Stewart and his following, and the good Douglas, who was so brave, fighting then in that mighty encounter, would say that those who pressed their foes' might so hard in that fight, defeating them wherever they went, were worthy of all honour. (194) There you could see many a steed fleeing riderless without a lord. Ah! Lord! [Anyone] who then paid attention to the good earl of Moray and his [men] who gave such mighty blows, and fought so hard in that battle, undergoing such toil and trouble that they and theirs made such an affray that wherever they came they made a way. (203) Then men could hear rallying cries, and Scotsmen shouting boldly, 'On them, on them, on them! They yield!' With that they attacked so hard, killing all they could overcome, and the Scottish archers also shot so swiftly among them, harassing them so grievously (210) that, what with those who were fighting against them, raining such mighty blows on them, pressing them so fiercely, and what with the arrows that made so many wicked wounds upon them, often slaying their horses also, they gave a little ground. (218) They feared dying then so greatly that their discipline got worse and worse, for those who were fighting against them set boldness, strength and will, and heart and courage too, with all their might and all their main, to put them utterly to flight.

(225) At this point that I am telling of just now, when that battle was being fought in this way, where on each side they were fighting vigorously, yeomen and boys and carters who had been left in the Park to guard the provisions, when they knew without doubt that their lords were fighting their enemies in desperate

combat, (234) made one of themselves, [of those] who were there, chieftain of them all, and fastened sheets that were fairly broad in place of banners upon long poles and spears, saying that they meant to see the fight, and help their lords to their utmost.

(241) When all had agreed to this, they gathered in one body – they were fifteen thousand or more – and then at great speed they went with their banners all in one force, as if they had been strong brave men. (247) They came with all that gathering to just where they could see the battle, then all together they gave a cry, 'Kill! kill! On them now!' and with that they were coming, although they were still far away. (253) The Englishmen who were giving ground by force of pressure, as I said before, when they saw coming towards them such a company, shouting like that, [a company] which they thought was at least as numerous as that fighting against them there, and which they had not seen before, [well,] you can believe without a doubt, that they were so badly disheartened, that the best, the bravest, who were in their army that day, wished that they were [somewhere else] with their honour. (265) King Robert saw from their pulling-back that they were close to defeat, and had his battle cry shouted, then with those of his company pressed his enemies so hard that they were so apprehensive that they gave ground more and more, for all the Scotsmen who were there, when they saw them escaping from the fighting, laid into them with all their might. (275) They scattered in sundry groups and were close to defeat; some of them fled openly, but those who were brave and bold, whom shame prevented from fleeing, kept up the struggle at great cost, standing firm in the fight.

(282) When the king of England saw his men fleeing in various places, and saw the enemy's army that had grown so brave and bold that all his folk were altogether so dismayed that they

lacked strength to withstand their foes in the encounter, (289) he was so greatly discouraged that he and his company [of] five hundred fully armed [men] in a mighty rush all took to flight and made towards the castle. (294) Yet I've heard some men say that Sir Aymer de Valence, when he saw the field almost lost, led the king away from the fighting by his rein against his will, and when Sir Giles d'Argentan saw the king and his company making to flee so speedily thus, he came swiftly right to the king and said, (303) 'Sir, since you mean to go [on] your way like this, [I] bid you good day, for I mean to [go] back; assuredly I never yet fled, and I choose to stay here and die, rather than to live in shame [by] flight'. (309) Without another [word] he turned his bridle, rode back and galloped at Sir Edward Bruce's force, which was so stout and unyielding, as though he had no fear of anything, shouting 'Argentan'. (315) They met him so with spears, and set so many spears upon him, that he and his horse were so pressed that both fell to earth and he was killed in that very place. There was great sorrow at his death, [for] in truth he was the third best knight who lived in his time known to men; he achieved many a fine feat of arms. (324) He fought three campaigns against the Saracens, and in each of those campaigns he defeated two Saracens. His great valour came to an end [in this battle].

(328) When Sir Aymer had fled with the king, there was none who dared remain, but [all] fled scattering in every direction, their foes pressing them hard. (332) Truth to tell, they were so terrified, and they fled in fear so fast, that a very great part of them fled to the River Forth and there most of them were drowned; Bannockburn between [its] banks was so filled with men and horse that men could then pass dry-foot over it on drowned horses and men.

Index